PLEASANT PERSISTENCE

YOUR KEY TO $ALES $UCCESS

DR. R. ANTHONY MATHENY

Performance Publishing Group
McKinney, TX

ISBN:
978-1-956914-95-5

CONTENTS

Note To Readers . . . ix
Foreword . . . xi
Introduction . . . xiii

1 Why Persistence? . . . 1
2 Persistence in Your Sales Mindset . . . 11
3 Persistence in Your Prospecting . . . 19
4 Persistence in Your Preparation . . . 25
5 Persistence in your Questioning . . . 33
6 Persistence in Discussing Benefits and Risks . . . 39
7 Persistence in Asking for the Sale . . . 45
8 Persistence in Overcoming Objections . . . 51
9 Persistence in Your Follow-Up . . . 63
10 Summary/Closing Comments . . . 75

How to Learn More From Dr. Matheny . . . 81

DEDICATED TO MY dad, Sanford C. Matheny—"Sandy"—who inspired me and everybody who knew him. Despite open heart surgery, treatment for three major cancers, and surviving a burst kidney, he never sat around feeling sorry for himself. He counted every day as a blessing and never got depressed. He taught me that with hard work and the right attitude, I can do anything I set my mind to.

I also dedicate this book to my wonderful family. They've supported me through all the highs and lows that life has thrown at me. My beautiful wife, Kathy, has always encouraged me to fulfill my dreams. She believed in me, consistently telling me that everything would work out in the end. My son, Collin, is a bright young man who I love to bounce ideas off. We both learn from each other immensely. My mother, Bonnie, has always been there to love and support me through all stages of my life. I'm blessed to have these wonderful people, as well as two great sisters, Sheri and Kim, in my corner. They've always provided a shoulder to lean on or an ear to listen when needed. I'm eternally grateful for my sweet stepmom, Joanne, whose laugh is contagious and makes me smile every time I hear it.

I've also been blessed to have wonderful in-laws, Tom and Jeannette Clarich, and a fantastic stepfather, Richard "Gabe" Gero. This group always treated me like one of their own children, and even though they have passed, I feel them with me in spirit every day.

NOTE TO READERS

This book contains opinions, suggestions, and ideas from the research and personal experiences of the author. The purpose is to inform, teach, and be helpful on the subject of sales training. The tips, techniques, and strategies described in this book may not be appropriate or suitable for everyone in all situations. Because everyone is different, application of these ideas cannot guarantee or warrant any specific results.

The buyer and reader of this book should understand that neither the publisher nor the author is giving any financial, accounting, legal, or any other professional advice or services. It is suggested and recommended that the reader seek the services of a trained professional before following any advice or drawing any conclusions from the book.

No guarantee or warranty can be made regarding the accuracy or completeness of the information represented here. The author and the publisher disclaim any responsibility for any loss, risk, liability, professionally or personally, which occurs as a result of, directly or indirectly, following any of the content of this book.

FOREWORD

"You can have everything in life you want if you will just help enough other people get what they want." – Zig Ziglar

ZIG BELIEVED THAT persistent consistency was the #2 reason for his success. (#1 was character and integrity). The difference between being persistent and having consistency is that consistency is when you have a worthy goal or objective and you work on it every day or as often as necessary, until you achieve it. Persistent, according to the Ziglar definition, means that every day you work on something, you do a little bit more than the day before, or a little differently than the day before. **Every day you up your game, get a personal best, or tweak it just a little bit.**

If you are in sales, you may need to make 50 calls a day in order to hit your sales goal. Consistency means you make 50 calls a day. Persistency means each day when you make the calls, you add something new to it, a new intro, a different question or a new voice inflection. **Your goal is to be just a tiny bit better than the day before.** Success in your business does require good habits, and those good habits are only possible with persistent consistency.

As a Dentist, Orthodontist, Oral Surgeon, Doctor, and Sales Professional you have an awesome moral responsibility. Your training, gifts and talents put you in a very unique position. When you examine someone, you can literally look into their future, and with a great degree of certainty, predict what type of pain and life challenges they will face, if they do nothing. Your job is literally to help people avoid pain and enjoy the best life possible. How awesome is that!

"But wait" you are thinking, "why is Sales Professional in the same line as Dentist, Orthodontist, Oral Surgeon, and Doctor?" Because you can be the best ____________ (you fill in the blank) in the world and if you don't make the sale because you have neglected your sales skills then you have failed morally by allowing the person who trusted you to leave and endure at a later time the pain you knew was coming.

OUCH! Did that last sentence touch a nerve? It should. I am a huge believer in what you do and the way you improve people's lives. The highly successful healthcare professionals I know truly care about and serve their patients and they understand that the ability to heal only comes after the sale. You shouldn't lose any sleep when someone rejects your treatment plan - unless - you didn't prepare and present the most compelling consultation possible. If you winged it and they said no, that should keep you up at night because you failed in helping them to avoid future pain.

Pleasant Persistence will help you help more people and allow you to focus on Why you do what you do which is, I believe, to help others live their best life possible. Here is even more good news: The more people you help the more all of your other Why's are taken care of. Imagine - the better your *Pleasant Persistence* is, the better the world is. Go change the world!

Tom Ziglar, CEO Ziglar, Inc.
Proud son of Zig Ziglar

INTRODUCTION

DR. TONY MATHENY has practiced dentistry for 32 years as of the writing of this book. He prides himself on providing top quality dentistry and keeping his patients as comfortable as possible. He believes if his patients have a good experience in his office, they will be far more likely to return and keep up with their needed dental appointments.

The one thing Dr. Matheny never enjoyed about practicing dentistry is the stress involved in the job. It's very stressful. He's felt forced to see a high volume of patients to cover the overhead and make enough profit to pay the bills and payroll. He knew there had to be a better way.

One day, Dr. Matheny took a course on sales training that had nothing to do with dentistry. He was reluctant to learn sales because he didn't want to come across like a car salesman—being pushy, aggressive, or high pressure. The course was a revelation. It was not about shady sales techniques. High morals and ethics were practiced, and those in the course were taught to sell from the heart, not the wallet—because you *really* care.

Dr. Matheny went on to study every course on sales training he could find. He read tons of top sales training books. He also became a Ziglar Legacy Certified Trainer and Coach. He applied all he learned to dentistry, and it worked like magic in his office. He couldn't believe how well it worked and how much it increased his case acceptance. He received great feedback from his patients on how thorough he was and how much they could tell he cared about them.

Dr. Matheny was able to raise his case acceptance to three times the national average. That's an increase of 300%! He was able to cut back the number of patients he had to see each day to reach his financial goals. This resulted in a lot less stress. He could spend more time with his patients, strengthening their rapport and further increasing the quality of the dentistry.

The sales techniques worked so well in Dr. Matheny's office, he felt compelled to share them with his colleagues around the world. That way, they too could have a more productive, less-stressed office—allowing patients to get more of the dentistry they wanted and needed. Dentists were not taught these techniques in dental school. Even today, very few people teach them. It blew Dr. Matheny's mind, especially considering how incredible and life-changing the skills could be for a dentistry practice. Now, Dr. Matheny feels a calling to help 10,000 dental offices in the next 10 years. He hopes yours will be one of them!

Everything Dr. Matheny teaches comes with the absolute highest regard for treating patients. He believes you should treat others the way *you* want to be treated. He never recommends anything if it is not in the best interest of the patient. He has **zero** tolerance for anyone who tricks, lies, or deceives anybody just to make a dollar. Doing so is **criminal**. He is proud of everything he shares with his patients, and he talks to them like he would a loved family member.

Dentists spend a lot of time and money becoming dentists. They deserve a fair return on that investment. Dentists work hard managing employees and their patients' dental care. If Dr. Matheny can help dentists get their patients to like and trust them, their dental services will be recommended more. In turn, the office will collect more, the dentist can see less patients and decrease stress, and more patients can get the work done they want. Everybody wins!

Dr. Matheny believes that learning professional sales training has been **by far** the top skill he has learned in his career. It has given him the biggest return on his investment in terms of courses or seminars he has taken. In this book, Dr. Matheny teaches the many great tips, techniques, and strategies that helped him achieve his success. He has left out any fluff, just teaching the absolute bare bones skills you need to learn to improve your case acceptance and progress in your journey towards sales mastery!

Rather than reading the whole book in one go, try to implement the strategies taught *as you read and learn them*. Remember, sales training takes time to implement—but the journey is well worth it! Dr. Matheny focuses on all the ways persistence helps you achieve better sales, but there are multiple other strategies you'll want to learn and implement to add more to your sales tool belt.

At the end of the book, you'll find ways of continuing your path to sales mastery. You'll also be directed to where you can learn more from Dr. Matheny—in the form of one-on-on coaching and an online video course that dives deep into this subject for maximum results.

It's easy to revert to old ways of doing things. Review these concepts often with your team, practice them regularly, and role play everything you learn consistently. If you do, you will see your results steadily improve. You will reap phenomenal rewards beyond your dreams.

CHAPTER 1

WHY PERSISTENCE?

"We are what we repeatedly do. Excellence, then, is not an act, but a habit." – Aristotle

AS I METICULOUSLY sought sales mastery this last decade, I obviously knew the importance of persistence. But I didn't realize just how important and relevant it was to sales success until the weekend I flew out to Dallas to film my sales training videos for my course, Doctor Sales Academy. (I developed this course for dentists—to teach them all the aspects of increasing case acceptance, and getting the patient to say "yes" and schedule and pay for their dental work.) Throughout two long days of shooting, as I poured out every great strategy I knew, the word I said more than any other was **persistence**. I became incredibly aware just how huge this concept was for success in selling. I knew immediately that it had to be the focus of my next book.

Why did I call this book "Pleasant Persistence," you ask? There are many ways of being persistent, some of which are negative. We have all been subject to the annoying salesperson who cares only about their best interest. They keep pestering us, refusing to take "no" for an answer. That type of persistence will drive people away from you. It will lower your rapport with your prospects and decrease your reputation.

In this book, I am referring to persistence in a positive, professional manner. Selling from the heart, not the wallet, out of genuine care for your prospect with high morals and ethics. That is selling with integrity! It boils down to treating people the way you want to be treated.

Pleasant persistence—when you are providing more information, giving more benefits, and approaching the situation from a serving mindset—will show your prospect how much you care. When you *aren't* following up five times a day and you *are* treating your prospect the way you want to be treated, you will impress them and make yourself stand out as knowledgeable and caring.

In this book, we will focus on the new art of selling. What makes people buy has been the same for centuries, but what *has* changed is our focus on serving first and selling second. The idea is to give *before* you receive, and to focus on serving the prospect in a friendly, genuine way. The emphasis is on helping them first and foremost and worrying about the money later. This form of selling shows the buyer how much we care about them.

Many of the examples in this book will be of me selling dentistry to my patients. Please understand, though, that these sales principles apply to anyone, selling anything, in any profession. As you read through the book, apply what you learn to your career. Practice every scenario, substituting your own profession into each example to make it relevant.

Sales mastery is not something you learn quickly and then master for the rest of your life. Just like when I went to dental school, I couldn't master dentistry in a semester (or even a year). Dental school was four years of lectures, hands-on courses, and clinical hours working on patients. We were first taught the basics, then built on that knowledge. We learned how to do a simple one-surface filling, then a single crown, then a larger bridge. Eventually we learned full mouth reconstruction. It was a process. But the learning didn't stop there. It was imperative that we continually take courses to stay informed on the latest and greatest techniques. We had to fine-tune our skills so we could offer the best dentistry has to offer.

We all do the best we can with the knowledge and experience we have. We also do what is comfortable to us. We must realize that change is uncomfortable. It takes us outside of our comfort zone. Being momentarily uncomfortable is worth it to achieve our goals and obtain the results we need for ourselves, our team, and our customers. While learning new skills, it can be easy to regress back to what we know as "easy" or "comfortable." We need to continually be reviewing what we should be doing. We must reinforce this information by placing it at the forefront of our brains.

As soon as we take our attention off our new skills, we go back to what we have always done. But if we remain persistent, we develop habits that make it easier for us to not forget what we should be doing. Thus, it's less likely we return to our old ways. Don't be fooled into thinking there is a point where you never have to review this information again. I've been studying and practicing sales training for at least 12 years. Still, every time I review these strategies, tips, and techniques with my team, my results shoot up the following week. Why? Because by teaching them, I remind myself of everything I should be doing. I become better because of it. So, always review and practice—it will be time well spent!

Learning how to sell is a process. There are no shortcuts. You must follow a very systematic and organized approach. In my dental office, this process begins when the patient calls our office and, hopefully, schedules an appointment. They then go to the treatment room, have their exam and x-rays, and are presented with their treatment recommendations. The more consistently we follow this proven process, the more consistent our results will be.

Be patient. Don't rush the process. If you push too much, too hard, or too soon, you may lose the opportunity. If you aren't willing to be pleasantly persistent, then you may walk away from your prospect too early, leaving an easy sale for the next salesperson your prospect visits.

To earn the right to present your product or service to a prospect, you first must show them how much you care about them. The prospect must see and feel that you are willing to do what it takes to earn their business. It takes time to develop a relationship of belief and trust. You can't be in a hurry. Realize that it's a process, and understand that to achieve your sales goals, it is not going to be "instant gratification."

Some people these days want "instant gratification" with everything. You can see the look of pain on their faces and hear the anguish in their voices when they have to wait. They want all the fruits of labor as far as money, nice cars, and houses. They want the ability to do what they want, but don't want to persist through the necessary steps to achieve it. They want a career that requires no preparation to succeed. Unfortunately, a career in sales does *not* allow this.

Being pleasantly persistent can be a game-changer. It helps a salesperson not assume that a prospect doesn't have any interest in their product or service. It encourages self-confidence. The sales call can become what it was supposed to be: an invitation for a prospect to learn more about the direct benefits of a salesperson's product or service. Finally, it allows the salesperson to find out if their prospect actually has a need for what they are proposing.

According to Forbes Magazine, 68% of people stop buying because of the seller's indifference. The buyer will take their business elsewhere because they feel undervalued. The art of persistence means having an unshakable belief that you can help your prospect. You want to be in-tune and able to communicate with your prospect in a way that is going to help them. They must recognize the value in buying from you.

Besides being passionate about your product or service, it is critical to connect what you offer to the passion of others. People will buy what you have available if they become passionate about your brand, product, or service. They will continue to come back. Passionate people make strong connections, and strong connections are great for business.

Most people are unfortunately not born with the persistence they need to be successful with sales. They must try to learn it. It doesn't come easy at first, but if they keep practicing and don't give up, they will see how effective being persistent is, and they'll become motivated to stay persistent. Knowing how to be persistent is just as important as being knowledgeable about the product or service you are selling. To become more persistent, you must continue developing good habits and trying to do more and more each week.

The biggest distinction between an average salesperson and an incredible one is persistence. Having persistence to make that first contact with your client, and then the discipline to make half a dozen more contacts (in a non-annoying way), is key. Once learned, practiced, and implemented, persistence can double or triple sales productivity. Persistence in sales can be summed up as the ability to continue when your natural instinct is to just give up and walk away.

Persistence is a part of every aspect of selling. Without it, there is no successful sales process! You've likely heard of the 80/20 rule. It says that in most organizations, 20% of the people make 80% of the income. In sales, it's more like 10% of salespeople make 90% of the money. What are they doing that the other 90% isn't? You got it—**they are being persistent**. Persistence is indeed the secret weapon used to dominate sales. I really like this quote from Zig Ziglar, one of the greatest salesmen and motivational speakers our country has ever seen: "Motivation fuels the attitude that builds the Confidence necessary to sustain the Persistence."

If you have two salespeople with the same skills, experience, product, and prices, the main difference may only be persistence. An old saying states, "You only start selling when the customer says, 'No.'" Another quote I wrote years ago is, "Until the client says, 'no,' assume it's a go." Translation: Keep going forward with the sale—remaining pleasantly persistent—until the client makes it clear they don't want or need what you have to offer.

The 2021 Sales Enablement Report, after studying thousands of people, showed that 80% of sales were made after the fifth contact with a potential customer. However, almost half (48%) of the salespeople gave up after just one contact with the person they tried selling to! One "No" scared them away for good. Because they gave up so soon, they only received 2% of the sales—obviously quite poor results. 73% of salespeople quit after not receiving a "Yes" after a second contact, giving them only 3% of the sales. 85% gave up after not closing the deal after the third attempt, giving them 5% of the sales. And a total of 90% of salespeople in this study gave up after the fourth contact, where 10% of sales were completed. For the lucky remaining 10% who persisted past the fourth contact, **80%** of the sales were made!

Those statistics are sad for the customer. Just when they have finally dealt with all the resistance building in their mind, when they've talked themselves into moving forward and purchasing the product or service that someone tried to sell them four times, there's nobody around to take the order. 90% aren't to be found. Already, you can see how persistence can double or triple a person's sales productivity. The secret weapon that the top 10% of salespeople possess is PERSISTENCE. If these statistics are not a motivating factor to have persistence, I don't know what is!

In a 2010 Selling Power article from Graham Roberts-Phelps, a study is mentioned that looked at a group of 100 cold-call prospects. This study found an average of 10 prospects will say "yes" and agree to see you, 10 will say "no" right away, 20 will ask you to call back, 50 will not be available, and 10 will want more information. To get more of these prospects to become clients, you need to be persistent. Call the 50 who were "unavailable" again. Make a note of the 30 that wanted more information and wanted to be called back, then follow up with them. Persistence here can double or even triple the productivity of your sales.

Why do 90% of salespeople quit so early? Some simply get busy working. They feel it is easier to move on to someone else rather than follow up on a prospect who initially shot them down. Others simply lack the discipline to continue making those follow up calls, emails, and in-person visits. They let business and life get in their way. It comes down to persistence—not only to make the first call, but to make five or six calls after that. All without annoying the prospect, of course.

At my dental office, I love it when patients from another office come in for second opinions. All the hard work has already been done for me. Someone else took the x-rays, did the exam, came up with solutions to the patient's problems, presented the treatment, and most likely provided an estimate. The patient probably objected in some way, perhaps saying the price was too high. After that, the office closed the case presentation, gave the patient a copy of their estimate, then told them to call if they changed their mind. They blew it by not being persistent.

Just because the patient brought up their concerns, doesn't mean they are not going to buy. That's where we go wrong! We assume that if they resist, they are not interested or have no ability to buy. Those conclusions are **wrong**. When patients come to my office for a second opinion, I briefly go over the benefits of doing the work, the risks of doing nothing, and then ask a closing question. Often, the case is then accepted. The first office could have gotten the case too, if they had simply stuck with the patient a little longer and addressed more of their concerns. By not being persistent, they left an easy sale for their competitor.

Most salespeople want to make the sale immediately. They want instant gratification and the rewards of making the sale as quickly as possible. Who doesn't, right? Unfortunately, it rarely works that way. You must have the patience necessary to complete the sales process. You must be willing to "romance the sale" through building trust and by not being in a rush. If you push too hard or fast, you may lose the opportunity. It takes a little time, but it's worth it to get a larger percentage to say "yes."

There are many reasons why a person may not buy right away. For instance, they may not be in a position to make a decision, may have had an unusual setback in their finances, are not sure they need or want the product or service, not sure you are the right person to get it from, or are overwhelmed or confused about what you are offering. The list goes on. Still, we must not give up early. We must remain persistent to get the sale.

This persistence makes you stand out in the mind of the client. Others would have given up. By being persistent, we are available when our client is ready to buy. They have not forgotten about us, because we have been so persistent along the way, in a caring and pleasant way.

It's gratifying to know that even when we hear three or four rejections from a client, the sale is far from over. In fact, we know at that point that we are *closer* than we have ever been to closing the sale. Rather than getting frustrated that we are putting in time and not getting the sale, we can be excited that we are (usually) getting very close. A complete shift in our attitude and emotions can alter how we operate as humans.

Next, we'll explore how important it is in sales to have the right mindset. It is the foundational basis for all we do!

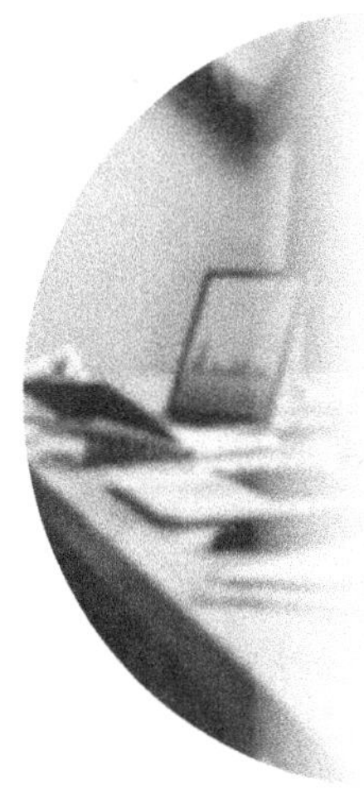

CHAPTER 2

PERSISTENCE IN YOUR SALES MINDSET

"Training and managing your own mind is the most important skill you could ever own, in terms of both happiness and success." – T. Harv Eker

BEING GREAT AT sales starts with adopting a positive mindset and taking small steps. You must commit to being persistent and consistent every day. You might not see immediate results, but over time (and by consistently taking action) you will build a foundation of sales success. Regardless of the business you are in, you have got to sell. That's not an easy thing to face for a lot of business owners. If you don't do it and do it well, it will be tough to stay in business for long.

Even if you do stay in business, you will struggle more than you need to. To survive and thrive, you've got to learn how to sell. Developing a great sales mindset means truly understanding that sales is a "process." It takes passion, believing in what you have to offer, and more than anything else, persistence!

Possessing the right sales mindset involves being clear on several traits. Sales leaders have these traits, and others do not. One is that they really have defined and understood their "Why?" It is one thing to understand "what" you do and "how" you do it—it's another to clearly understand "why" you do what you do. It's crucial to know exactly how your product or service will help your customer gain a benefit or avoid a loss. They realize they are not just selling; they realize they are **helping**.

As a salesperson, you must know why you are doing the work you are doing. Get away from the thought that you are working just to make money. By focusing on what that money will do for you—such as help you reach your goals and achieve your dreams, or provide you the freedom to do what you want or the ability to help others—you'll find added motivation. Concentrating on how you will be helped and how your potential client will benefit will make all your hard work worthwhile in the end. And you won't mind getting up in the morning to go do your job!

Sales leaders also have the mindset trait of helping and serving their client or customer from the very beginning. Nowadays, customers are knowledgeable and savvy. They also are skeptical due to all the scam artists trying to take advantage of people and steal their money. Your customer doesn't want to make a bad buying decision. If they ever feel that you, as the salesperson, has *your* best interest at stake and not *theirs*, they will immediately seek business elsewhere.

Here's an example. When I first started working as a dentist after dental school, I went to a car lot to look at possibly buying a new car. I found a car I liked and told the salesman that I needed to check into a couple things to see if I could buy it. I said I'd let him know soon. He then stated, "If you could get back to me by 5:00 p.m. today, that would be best. It's the end of the month, and I'm trying to win a contest for most cars sold." That rubbed me the wrong way. He clearly had his own interests ahead of mine. I never went back, and instead I ended up buying a new car a week later at another dealership.

Another sales mindset trait of great sales leaders is their ability to ask thorough questions, then listen to the responses. I'll dive more in detail on this in upcoming chapters, but for now, realize that salespeople make it their mission to serve their customers the best way they can. To do this, they must understand their customer. This includes knowing what the priorities for your customer are, what they want and need, and what they *don't* want and need. It involves learning about their situation, problems, and challenges so you can customize your service or product to best fit the client in front of you in the most beneficial way.

Many professionals, especially doctors, don't believe they are in sales. However, anytime you are exchanging your products or services for money, that **is** sales, whether you like it or not! You are always selling—selling your office, your team, yourself as the doctor, and your products and services. My business coach, Howard Partridge, would say, "Nothing happens in a business until a sale is made." This is so true! We can't help any of our patients or clients, while also surviving as a business, if we can't sell. Learning to sell is paramount to the success of any business. Sales is like oxygen—without it, businesses would die.

Most dentists don't look for help with sales training, even though they have never been taught anything about the subject. There are two reasons for this. One, they don't realize they have a problem with sales conversions, or what they call, "case acceptance," because they either don't track it at all or don't track it accurately. The second reason is that they believe we, as dentists, shouldn't be selling anybody anything in the healthcare profession, feeling it is unprofessional or unethical. They believe we should just educate the patient, and those that want the treatment will take it. This reasoning couldn't be further from the truth. If this logic was true, the acceptance rate for patients paying and scheduling for treatment wouldn't be 25% nationwide.

Selling—especially in health professions—is considered a bad word. It has a negative reputation. When most hear the word "sell," they think of a pushy, aggressive salesperson, like an insurance salesman who is applying high pressure to make a sale. It is obvious that he or she has **their** own best interest at stake, not **yours**. Yes, that type of selling does exist, but the only kind of selling that I believe in and teach is to sell what's best for your client, not your collections.

You are suggesting things you would want yourself. This is truly selling with integrity! Let's put any negative thoughts we have had in the past about selling or salespeople aside, and instead realize you don't ever have to resort to shady sales tricks. The selling and strategies in this book are ones you can be proud of, not embarrassed about.

It's interesting that those working in health professions are resistant to learn sales training. They don't want to appear pushy or aggressive, yet the percentage of their patients that say "yes" to the services they are offering is low, around 25-30% (according to the American Dental Association). Why is that number so low? Because we are coming across to patients as pushy or aggressive, caring more about the sale and making money than we do about their specific needs or wants. You see, without comprehensive sales training, we as a profession are not building the trust and rapport with patients that they need to feel comfortable. Without comfort, they won't buy.

When we don't take the time to find out what they need and want, show how much we care about them, and properly deal with all the resistance, concerns, and objections they have, we'll be perceived by the patients as more interested in making the sale than doing what is best for them. You see, we are avoiding sales training because we feel we shouldn't be selling in healthcare. We don't want to appear high pressure, yet we are already being perceived as that *without us even knowing.* It is my life's mission to change this old-fashioned way of thinking and show dentists and others how they can get better results, increase their quality of life, have the time to perform better work, and help more people.

Professional sales training teaches us how to build the trust and confidence people need to go forward working with you. You learn how to ask the proper questions needed to customize your presentation to a specific potential client. By doing so, you really pique their interest and desire. They feel that you are really listening to them and that you care about doing what is best for them.

Sales training teaches you not to get frustrated with your client when they don't immediately agree to the product or services you are suggesting. You learn that people need to hear something several times before they buy. You figure out that objections are not necessarily a bad thing. They can be a sign of interest or a need to clarify some points you brought up. You are taught to help your client overcome all the natural resistance that goes on in their brain. This allows them to feel comfortable enough to trust in you and what you are selling. They can move forward and buy what you are proposing.

The funny thing about sales training is that it allows you to be *less* pushy, aggressive, and high-pressure in the eyes of your prospect, because the prospect feels how empathetic and compassionate you are. You have built that rapport and trust with them. Your approach will be the *opposite* of what everybody thinks!

Is that because I am being perceived as pushy or aggressive? No! It is the exact opposite! If I was being perceived as such by my patients, my case acceptance rate would be less than average, not 300%

higher, right? My patients tell me frequently that they can tell how much I care about them. They say nobody has taken this much time with them before. These feelings build the rapport and trust they require to choose me as their dentist.

It's ironic how we, as doctors, avoid learning sales training to not appear too pushy, when, in reality, sales teach us how *not* to be pushy. Even without the sales aspect, our profession is often perceived as pushy or money-driven. I find it funny how our sale percentages are low, and we blame it on everything and everybody else, without recognizing the true cause. We blame the bad economy, the fact that our patients don't have a high dental IQ, or our patients for not having enough money. Or we blame other dentists for competing with us in our local area, or the number of corporate chains popping up. Granted, these excuses can be valid to some extent. They affect business to a degree. But learning to sell *ethically* can overcome any such problems. We fail to realize that learning about what makes people buy or not buy could dramatically help us. And by improving our sales techniques, we can in turn help a lot more people than we are right now.

I recognize the fact that continuing to "hang in there" with a potential client is uncomfortable, especially when they don't seem interested. However, you must realize that being persistent is what makes sales! I'll often ask others, "Do you want to be comfortable and poor? Or would you rather be a little uncomfortable and reach your financial goals?" Think about it. Change is uncomfortable, but it's well worth it!

There are many reasons people buy and many reasons why they *don't* buy. I'm sure there is a lot of complicated science behind what goes on in our mind when someone tries to sell us something, why we initially resist, and why it takes a certain level of exposure to something before we feel comfortable enough to proceed with the sale. I don't want to bore you or confuse you with all the psychology or neuroscience behind all of this. It's simply important for us to know and believe how we are wired as human beings.

In other words: What do we need to hear to feel comfortable to buy? And what makes us not buy? If, for example, we know that all we need is time to process the idea of buying something, to deal with all the resistance that is going on in our brains, then we are more likely to hang in there with the client or patient. We'll be more persistent, letting them work through the resistance going on in their head before they eventually say "yes."

Even though we know how important it is to be persistent, that doesn't mean it is easy to keep going once you hear a "no" or get your first objection. Many people fall into the mindset that the client is rejecting them as a person, rather than rejecting the product or service. Nobody likes rejection. It is human nature to fear rejection. But you must remember that failure is a reflection of an event, not of the person. Don't take it personally.

Remember, it's normal for your client to reject your offer the first few times they hear it. If you keep that in mind, you'll be less likely to get upset or bothered by the rejection. In fact, each time I hear a "no" or get an objection from a client, I remind myself, "Good, I'm one step closer to getting that 'yes.'" When you have that mindset, you won't be bothered by objections as much. It will be easier for you to persist and find a way around the objection.

We need to get rid of the mindset that if a potential client objects or says "no," it means they are not interested in our product or service. Being pleasantly persistent can truly make all the difference. It can allow your sales call to be an invitation for your client to learn about the direct benefits of your product or service. What's more, you can find out if they really need what you are offering. This is what your sales call should be about.

I realize that being persistent after meeting resistance is not always easy, but great salespeople push through their discomfort. They don't give up. They stay the course until they have achieved their goals. Keep telling yourself that most of your sales will be made between the fifth and twelfth attempt. This way, you won't become frustrated as much. Remember: nearly 90% of salespeople only make three attempts (or less).

If you find yourself getting aggravated, it's okay to vent. But when you're done, remind yourself of your past successes, like when someone didn't buy what you were selling right away and how it took you several attempts to get through to them. Remember how they finally came around, bought what you had, and became a happy, raving fan.

Having a persistent mindset is nothing more than being determined to be successful no matter what obstacles and challenges are thrown at you. You must remain committed to learning the habit of maintaining a steady course in both quality and activity. If you are persistent, you will achieve it. If you are consistent, you will keep it. If you commit yourself to being "consistently persistent," I promise your sales will increase significantly.

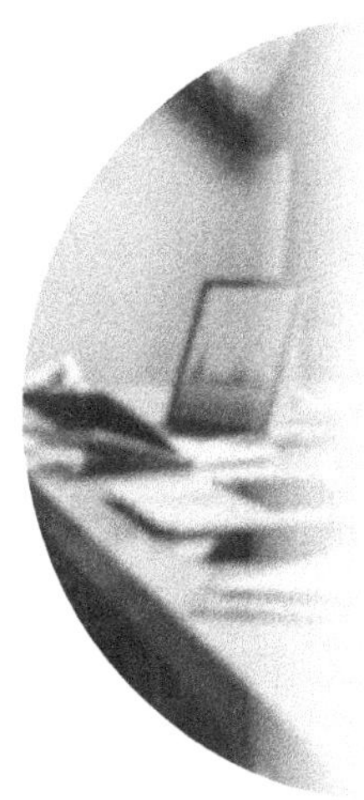

CHAPTER 3

PERSISTENCE IN YOUR PROSPECTING

"Energy and persistence conquer all things." – Benjamin Franklin

MOST SALESPEOPLE AND businesses need to be constantly prospecting. Doing so will help you add more prospects to your pipeline and give more sales presentations, thus generating more sales. Granted, there are certain high-demand businesses that can stay busy year-round through word of mouth or repeat business (these situations are more the exception than the rule). It is imperative that you learn to be persistent by prospecting at all times—not just when business slows down.

When a business is busy, they likely won't be prospecting for potential customers as much. And if they don't, they tend to run out of paying customers at some point. There tends to be a lag between when you start prospecting and the time these customers start doing business with you. If you only prospect when slow times occur, you'll have four-six weeks of slow times until the prospecting starts to pay off. By persistently prospecting—even when your business is busy—your revenue won't be so cyclical with high up and down months. It'll be more level and consistent.

I am surprised to hear of so many businesses that do no prospecting for new clients. They feel that just hanging their sign outside their business or having a website will attract enough new business.

Granted, there are some businesses that have a long-standing track record of always staying busy through word-of-mouth referrals, and they don't have to do any other prospecting. But these places are rare.

For the rest of us, persistent prospecting is crucial. Businesses need two things to not only survive, but thrive: marketing and sales. Marketing (prospecting) must be done for prospects to find out where you are, who you are, and what services you offer. Once they come into your place of business, sales expertise is needed to convert these prospects into clients. One without the other is not very effective.

You might bring a lot of people into your business—but if your conversions are low, it will be tough to have great success. On the other hand, you may be a sales master, but if you don't have enough people to sell what you have to offer, production and collection numbers will be low. But if you do well with *both* concepts, you will have the formula for a wonderful, successful business. The sky will be the limit!

I would always attempt to be doing some type of promotion or marketing effort to attract new patients and reactivate existing patients who hadn't visited the office for a while. I would ramp the promotion up and increase it six weeks prior to sections of the year that have typically been slower.

For example, in my office, August and September tend to be the slowest months of the year. So, I would greatly increase my marketing efforts between the middle and end of June, knowing that it takes at least four-six weeks for those efforts to pay off. This would help regulate our cash flow, so we'd avoid the extreme high and low months. It is so tempting to slow down or stop prospecting for new clients when you are super busy—but if you don't want to run out of work, you have to keep going.

Prospecting includes anything you do to attract customers. It can be internal marketing, where you promote to your existing customer base to either get them to do more business with your company or ask them to refer people they know.

Prospecting can also involve external marketing where you attempt to market to new prospects via phone calls, in-person visits, direct mail postcards, flyers, billboards, and more. This also includes all types of ads from radio, television, and social media-sponsored ads on Facebook, Twitter, LinkedIn, or YouTube.

In my dental office, we made up referral cards we called "Care Enough to Share" cards. The card had our contact information on it and—more importantly—a special offer for the new potential patient receiving the card. It had two lines on it to be filled out. One was for the name of the patient handing the card out to their friend or family member. The other line was to be filled out by the person receiving the card.

We instruct our patients to tell the person receiving the card to make sure they bring the card into the office. And when they do, we honor the special offer on the card. We also know the name of the patient who gave them the card. We can now thank and reward the referring patient, which encourages him or her to continue handing out more cards marketing our office.

Our office would also buy a special prize (a big screen TV, BBQ grill, cookware set, etc.) every quarter of each year. We'd announce on flyers in the office, on our website, and all over social media that we are holding a referral contest. For every referral a patient made that *came into the office,* we put a ticket in the jar. The winner was drawn the end of a three-month period. And you know what happened with each of these giveaways? The referrals from our patients brought in much more revenue than the cost of the prizes!

Reaching out to people who have not been in for a while is usually more successful than reaching out to new people who know nothing about you. People who have been referred to you, then came in and had a good experience at your office, are easier to get back in than a stranger who has yet to form a relationship with your team.

Most businesses need new clients. I'm not discouraging promoting to new people, but I recommend doing it *after* you've reached out and marketed to your existing clients. You need to check in with the ones that haven't been into your business for a while. Market to them other services you have to offer, which they may not be familiar with. Then ask for referrals (family members, friends, neighbors, co-workers, etc.) who may be able to benefit from the products or services your company offers.

Generally, people don't mind calling people they know, but they tend to really hate reaching out to people or businesses they have never met. This is the dreaded **cold call**! Salespeople often are unsure of what to say during a cold call without sounding sleazy, pushy, or desperate for business. They feel awkward. This feeling—along with the fear of rejection—makes many salespeople limit their cold calling.

When you reach out to a new prospect in person or over the phone, it is best to say hello, then state your name and the company you represent. At this early juncture, avoid any other arbitrary conversation. Next, state the purpose of your call and why the person you're talking to might benefit from your business.

For example, if I was calling a new dentist to offer coaching or training, I would say something like, "Hi, Dr. Smith, I'm Dr. Matheny.

I wanted to introduce you to my case acceptance mastery program, which can help you double the number of patients that say 'yes' to your treatment recommendations without you being pushy or aggressive or having to spend any more money on advertising. Dr. Strawn—a dentist whose office I recently trained—saw an increase of 25% in their collections the very month after I trained them. Would you be interested in hearing more about this?"

If they respond with a positive answer, I would then see if now is a good time or if it would be best to set up a time another day. I would prefer to meet in person or on a video call. If neither is possible, I'll talk over the phone as a second choice. If you set up a future time with a potential client, suggest a day and time, such as, "How is Wednesday at 2:00 p.m.?" This is better than giving them multiple choices. If they have a conflict with what you suggested, they will say so.

My best advice is to remember a few key points. One, when your prospect says "no," they are not rejecting you personally, they are just saying, "Now is not a good time for me." It is just a temporary "no." Second, you must realize that this is all a numbers game. You might call 20 people before hearing your first "yes."

That may seem like a failure to some, but to me, it's still a success. Through this lens, if you call 60 people, you'll have 3 new clients. If you call 100, you will get 5 new customers, which can equate to hundreds or thousands of dollars in income for your company.

One more point to keep in mind. When you cold call, do it from a *serving* standpoint. Have the mentality that you genuinely care about the person you are calling. Act as if they are a loved one you are trying to help. Prospects can hear and feel the compassion and empathy in your voice. So, believe in your product, and feel good about how your product or service can make your prospect's life better, happier, easier, wealthier, etc. If you believe in your product enough, your potential client will too.

I hope you realize—now more than ever—that persistent and consistent prospecting is key to having a continuous flow of customers in your pipeline. With consistent prospects, you can always be marketing and selling your services or products. As you have learned, this needs to be done non-stop, whether your business is slow or busy, to avoid ups and downs.

Next, we will address why your sales success relies on being persistent with your sales preparation.

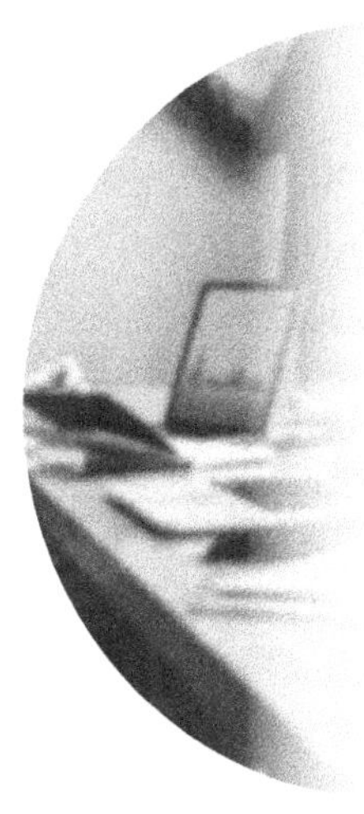

CHAPTER 4

PERSISTENCE IN YOUR PREPARATION

"Success seems to be connected with action. Successful people keep moving. They make mistakes but they never quit." – Conrad Hilton

FOCUS AND CONSISTENCY are accomplished with proper preparation, planning, and practice. Sales professionals self-reflect and use consistent action to prepare every day. They ask themselves, "What action do I need to do today to achieve my goal?" or "What actions and activities do I need to repeat to achieve my goal?" They have a clear understanding of which activities to repeatedly complete. They take action.

A lack of planning can lead to being inefficient, wasting time, mounting frustrations, and most of all a low return on your investment of time spent with your prospect. Being persistent with your preparation, on the other hand, can lead to more confidence for the person doing the presentation and ultimately lead to higher sales success. In your preparation, always be thinking about how your product/service can either solve a problem or achieve a goal that your prospect needs.

What are some things you can do to prepare before you meet with your client/customer/patient? Hopefully, if you met and talked with your prospect previously, you have some notes about what they are interested in. "What is their main concern?" should be the top of your list. If you're unsure, make a note to find out as soon as possible. Doing a little research about your prospect or their business can go a long way in building rapport and making your product or service more relevant for their situation.

The first question to answer is this: What is the best product, service, or treatment plan for this person (which you've calculated based on your interview with them or your examination of them)? Once you've answered this question, figure out before you meet with your client exactly what the investment will be and what payment options are available for them, if they are wanted or needed.

Next, you must be prepared to explain what you are recommending for the client, what's involved in the process, how much time it will entail, and any other details involved in performing your service or delivering the product. Figure out what benefits the clients will get if they invest in your product or service. Remember, don't only think about the obvious practical benefits—plan out any emotional benefits as well, such as how they will look or feel younger, be more confident, have more self-esteem, etc. It is a known fact that people buy based on emotions, then justify their purchase based on facts.

Determine all the options available to help your prospect accomplish their goals, needs, or wants. Then, prepare to present the BEST of those options. I believe it is important to figure out all the options available, but I am not a fan of presenting all of them. Why? Because it can be confusing and overwhelming when someone is presented with so many choices at once. People don't want to make a bad buying decision. They will often be compelled to say they have to "think about it" or "talk to their spouse" to review and process all the information given to them. A famous saying in sales is, "Confused people don't buy." Throughout my career, I've determined this adage to be true.

Your first thought hearing this might be: "Wait a minute, not everybody is going to want or be able to get their most ideal option. What about those people?" During your preparation, always figure out the second or third best options as well. That way, you're covered if someone doesn't want the first option. If a prospect expresses that the most ideal choice is not for them, I will happily explain other available options. But why bother spending time going into these other options and risk confusing them (or being overwhelmed entirely, thus choosing nothing) when the first choice is something they want to do, *and* it fits into their budget?

During your preparation, in advance of the presentation, figure out all the challenges or problems your product/service can or will solve for them. This will make your prospect aware of more opportunities that can be improved upon.

Also, determine the risks involved if they decide *not* to invest in your product or service. Don't ever skip this step. The risk of loss is more motivating than the benefit of gain. By being persistent with your preparation, you won't forget to include any of the important aspects that are crucial for your sales success. And you won't be stuck trying to come up with all these things on the spot with the prospect in front of you. Being organized in advance will make the presentation more efficient and improve how you are perceived by the prospect.

Your clients must understand not only *why* they need your product/service, but also that they need it *now*. Determine in advance why it is important for them to buy your product or service. Stressing **urgency** is valuable. It is human nature for us to put off buying anything until we really have to, especially if it's something we don't enjoy (like having dental work done). Having dentistry done is something not many people look forward to. If someone can put off spending the money and dealing with some discomfort, they will—as long as they believe it won't cause any serious problems and turn into an emergency. In my dental office, it is our job to express urgency if someone is in need of pressing dental work. Figuring this out in advance will greatly increase the odds of someone agreeing to what you propose.

People relate well to stories. We all love stories, especially ones that grab our attention. Figure out ahead of your presentation any stories you can tell that relate to the needs of your client or to the product/service you are suggesting. Providing social proof or testimonials for your client/patient goes a long way in building trust. You can do this by relaying a story of a similar client (to your current client). Explain how a similar client looked and felt before they invested in your product/service versus how they looked or felt after they invested in your product/service. People are more likely to agree to purchasing a product or service if other people before them have made the purchase and seen beneficial results. Take the time to prepare stories in advance that apply to your prospect. It's hard to think of relevant stories on the spot during a sales presentation.

Showing that others received great benefits after buying from you is crucial. Doing so allows new prospects to trust you enough to invest in what you have to offer. Gather any testimonials you have from happy existing clients, and then be prepared to show them during the sales presentation. One tip that really helped me: Remember to ask for testimonials when someone is happy or gives you a compliment about the service provided. Here's another tip: Organize those testimonials in a folder or binder arranged according to the service or product you sell. In my office, I have testimonials grouped together for patients happy with dentures, crowns or bridges, whitening, and dental implants. This way, when I'm preparing for a consultation, I can easily grab one or two relevant testimonials and have them handy for the presentation.

You should also determine **ahead of time** what questions you want to ask your client during the sales presentation. Also, anticipate what questions or objections your prospect will have for you. Plan out how you will answer these questions and ask yourself if your answers will be well-received. If you've been in your field for a while, you'll become familiar with the most common questions asked. When you incorporate the answers to these questions or concerns during your talk, it makes it easier for your prospect to commit to what you are offering them. If their concerns, questions, and objections are all answered in a satisfactory way before the end of your presentation, they'll be left little reason to say "no."

Based on what you are recommending to your potential client, compile any visual aids that would help explain or demonstrate further details about the product or service. These can include photographs, physical models, educational videos, or any pamphlets or brochures. The saying "a picture is worth a thousand words" is so true. Showing before and after pictures can make somebody want your service or product even more. In my office, we have educational videos on all types of dental procedures that explain what we are proposing in a 3-D manner. Anything that helps your potential client visualize what is possible also helps eliminate confusion and motivate them to go forward.

Your prospect will usually not notice if you do **not** prepare for a sales presentation, but they will surely notice if you **do** prepare. They will be thoroughly impressed, and you will be perceived as an organized and competent individual, as someone with their act together. Being prepared allows you to be confident going into the sales presentation because you have spent time to become thoroughly aware of all aspects of your prospect's situation. Your prospects can tell if you're confident. They will feel more comfortable buying your service or product.

During your presentation, if you detail and address the most common objections or resistance points that your prospective customer could have, they'll be left with nothing to object to! If you've answered all their concerns, getting a "yes" becomes much easier.

Nowadays, we're all busy all the time. Preparing for a presentation is the part of the sales process that is most neglected. I often hear people say, "As doctors, we don't have that much time to adequately prepare for every case presentation the way you are suggesting." I understand that, but a lot of what we discussed can be delegated to your assistants. You can give them a copy of the patient's treatment plan before the consult or case presentation. Then they can prepare models, videos, or necessary brochures, along with applicable testimonials.

For small treatment plans (such as the filling of a crown or two), very little preparation is required. For a larger plan that involves a lot of steps, many procedures, and a higher cost, more time needs to be spent preparing. Also, more time must be spent *during* the actual presentation with the client. These variables are based on each individual case.

Dentists often ask me, "How can you afford to spend the time you do preparing for the case presentation when you aren't getting paid for that time?" My answer? Because it increases the number of patients who accept, pay, and schedule for their treatment. Really, I can't afford *not* to spend this time. If spending an extra 30-60 minutes per day at no charge allows me to fill my day with more productive procedures, it's worth it.

The same holds true for giving no-charge consults to clients to discuss treatment. Dentists wonder how I can afford to spend so much time with patients at no charge. It's because I sell three times the amount of dentistry at my consults than the average dentist. To make my point, I've asked dentists what scenario they like better: working hard at the chair doing neck- and back-breaking dentistry all day to produce $3,000-$5,000 with no consults, or producing $10,000 in the morning and spending the afternoon doing no-charge consults (and then preparing for consults to sell another $10,000 in dentistry the next morning)? Seems like a no-brainer to me!

In this chapter, you've learned the importance of preparing for your presentation. We've also discussed the benefits of preparing for a presentation in advance of meeting with your prospect or patient. If you are going to take the time and effort to do a presentation, you might as well give yourself and your prospect the highest odds of success in obtaining what you have to offer. This way, you'll achieve your desired results.

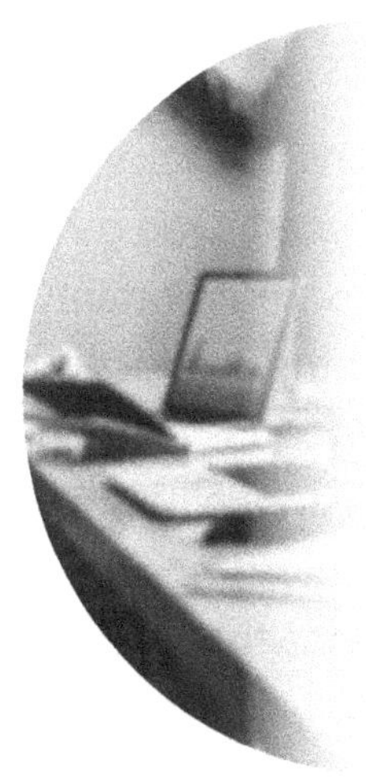

CHAPTER 5

PERSISTENCE IN YOUR QUESTIONING

"Failure is often the line of least persistence." – Zig Ziglar

ASKING QUESTIONS IS crucial in sales. Within two days of your conversation with a client, they will remember 75% of what **they** said, but only 34% of what **you** said. That's why it is so crucial to ask questions and get them talking. Try to have your client talk, as much as, if not more, than you do. This will significantly bolster your relationship with the client.

Just like an attorney in a courtroom, asking questions puts you in charge of the conversation. When you ask questions, the client will view you as an ally. It becomes obvious by your questions how much you care about them.

When you ask people questions, you start to form a business friendship. People like to do business with someone they know, especially a new or old friend. When you ask several questions, it builds rapport. People love to talk about themselves. Sharing information back and forth allows you and your prospect to establish some common ground. An example of this would be if you and your prospect like the same sports team, or if you're both dog lovers. You realize you have things in common and chat about these interests, which in turn increases your odds of securing their business.

So, what should you ask them? The relevant questions you ask will depend on the product or service you are selling. In general, you can basically survey the client to see what benefits or features are important to them. For example, you can ask if the longevity of the product is important to them, if the cost is a concern, if noise is important, or how much money or time it will save them. Whatever their answer is, you can respond with, "Tell me more about that," to get more valuable information from the client. Ask open-ended questions that probe for more information—not just "yes" or "no" questions.

Here's why it's crucial to ask your prospect questions: you'll find out what **they** feel is important to **them**. You can then customize your presentation to what is important to **them**. The moment you start discussing with a client something **they** feel they don't want or need, they will shut you out. The likelihood of them buying from you plummets.

We often go over benefits with clients, but it is very important not to go over benefits until you know which ones are important to each specific client. As soon as you start discussing benefits the client feels they don't need or want, then they will tune you out and quit paying attention to your presentation.

When you start going over anything the prospect feels would not apply to them, they feel as if your talk is a generic, not customized to them. They feel you're not touching enough on their wants or needs.

This process can also be a big timesaver for you. There might be, for example, 10 advantages for the client to buy the product or service from you. If the client is only interested in four of the advantages, there is no need to discuss the other six. This saves you time, and the client gets the information and facts they care about. Both parties win!

For example, if I have an elderly man in my dental chair and I start discussing with him the teeth whitening procedure we do in the office, how it works, the great results he will get, and the cost, I may lose him at some point along the way. If his main concern is not losing any teeth or just having the ability to chew his food well, the color of his teeth may be of no concern to him!

Why would I waste my time going into all the details of whitening if it is something **he feels** he doesn't need? All that does is waste everyone's time.

How do you find this out ahead of time? By being persistent with your questioning! I could have simply asked, "Mr. Jones, are you concerned with the color of your teeth?" If he says that he could care less about how they look, I know I can move on to talking about other issues that are more relevant to him.

In my dental office, I would often ask if the patient would like to just handle their current emergency, or if they'd like to get their whole mouth put into a state of health. I would ask if they have any pain or if they are concerned about the procedure or cost. That way, I'd learn about their biggest fears or concerns.

You can also answer the client's question with a question of your own. For example, if they ask about cost, you can ask them, "Is the cost of this product/service something you are concerned about?" Usually they say "yes." However, sometimes they will say "no" and state that they were simply curious about cost.

You can also ask your client to rate their priorities from 1-10 regarding how important each of the following things are: beauty, function, comfort, and longevity. These items fit well for my patients in the dental office, but obviously you can take out any that don't apply to you and substitute ones that better fit what you are selling.

Here's another strategy. Say to your client, "If you had a magic wand and could change anything about yourself (new car, suit, the teeth in your mouth, etc.), what would you change?" Then, hopefully, you'll be able to tell them ways your service or product can help improve what they have been dealing with.

You can end this part of the conversation with your client by asking them if you've answered all their questions. There may be one or two questions they have been sitting on that you never addressed. It's best to handle those concerns immediately.

By being persistent, by asking questions to learn and understand the prospect's underlying problems, the prospect will know that you understand them, and they will be loyal to you because of the trust you've established. They likely won't go to anyone else because they will doubt that anyone else will be as committed as you have been. As a rule of thumb, the harder the client is to get, the harder it is to lose them. That's because this type of client requires a lot of persistence—the kind most salespeople don't have.

If you follow this advice and remain persistent with questioning of your potential client—probing to find out everything that is a concern and leaving out everything that is not a concern—you will see your prospect become highly interested and engaged in the conversation. They are going to feel that you have really listened to them and tailored your presentation to them. Your chance of closing the sale will rise significantly.

Most people don't take the time to ask enough questions or the *right* questions. Everyone is in a hurry in our busy society. Questioning is such a crucial step—ask plenty of questions before you do your sales presentation, and you'll reap the benefits!

Now that you know how to ask questions and the importance of doing so, you must learn to be a good **listener**. Many salespeople are so busy and focused on what they have to say to their prospect, they don't give the prospect a chance to respond, express their needs and wants, and say what is truly important to them. If you listen close enough, the prospect will often tell you what they need to hear from you before they finally decide to buy your product or service.

Active listening allows you to learn what motivates your client. You can learn what they need or want, then close the sale. In my dental office, I once had a patient tell me, "If you tell me I need to do this treatment and I need to do it now, I'll do it." That was her way of telling me that it had to be urgent for her to get it done. It was urgent. I repeated back to her what she told me to say, and then she signed up, paid, and scheduled to do the work. If only all clients made it this easy for us by telling us what they need to hear before buying.

Questions also help you isolate the patient's objections. They help you establish a long-term relationship and further rapport with your client.

Some good rules of thumb for proper listening include: not interrupting your prospect when they are talking, not trying to finish their sentences, and having them elaborate by probing them for more information. Also important: listening for what is implied or spoken between the lines, being completely present, not having your mind on something else so you can listen very intensely, and not prejudging when you listen.

Maintaining good eye contact, sitting eye-to-eye, and giving verbal cues, such as, "Oh," "Huh," or "Wow," will let them know you are paying attention. You can also restate some of the sentences or points your prospect made when they were speaking to show them you truly understood what they were saying. The most important statement I have ever heard or read about effective listening came from Jeffrey H. Gitomer, "Listen with the intent to understand ... *before* you listen with the intent to respond."

Even though listening is crucial in the sales process, it is often a fairly weak or absent trait with people. I call active listening the First Commandment in sales. You have learned the importance of asking questions and what to ask, but it won't yield the benefits you are looking for if you don't listen well.

Oftentimes, people ask a question but are thinking of their *next question* while their client is speaking. This causes them to neglect valuable information. Remember, nobody has ever listened their way out of a sale, but they sure have talked their way out of one! If you listen intently and watch your prospect's actions, they will help tell you how to act, what to say, and what not to say. This will lead to a faster sale.

Next, I'll bring you one step closer to sales wizardry by helping you master the art of discussing benefits of your product or service for the client. I'll also help you explain the risks the client will face if they don't obtain your product/service. These strategies are imperative to motivate your prospect to say "yes" to what you are offering. Make sure you always include these in your presentation.

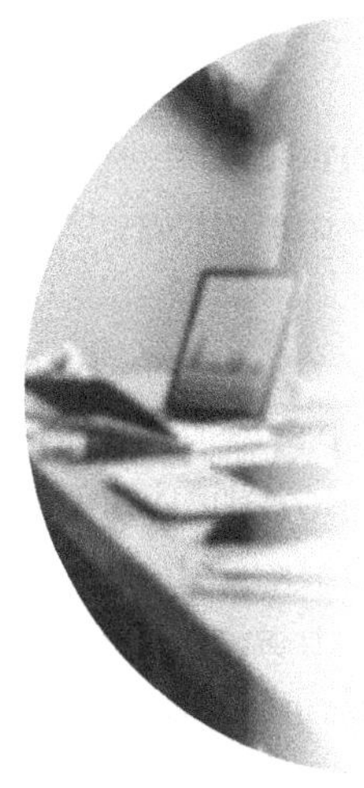

CHAPTER 6

PERSISTENCE IN DISCUSSING BENEFITS AND RISKS

"Do everything with character and integrity and practice persistent consistency in everything you do." – Tom Ziglar

BEING PERSISTENT WITH discussing the benefits of the product or service you are offering is critical for getting new clients. There are two types of benefits for clients that we will discuss in this chapter. I'll also explain the importance of discussing and presenting the risks of the client doing nothing (not buying your product or service). I often see salespeople explaining the benefits more than the risks. If anything, it should be the other way around.

A lot of these concepts overlap and affect each other. With this chapter, I'd like you to keep in mind that it is imperative to nail all the previous steps in the book before moving on to discussing benefits/risks. By doing so, we can learn beforehand what benefits our client is concerned about, what his or her main concern is, and what things they aren't concerned about.

By learning this, we will only be discussing the benefits important to our client. We won't be wasting time covering what's not important to them. In this chapter, assume that I am only talking about covering benefits that the client has already told me they are interested in or concerned about. Our prospect will be impressed that we listened and have customized our presentation to fit their wants and needs. We will have their full attention, which will solidify our efforts to make the sale.

Position yourself as a "problem fixer" rather than just a salesperson. There is a big difference between presenting information and delivering solutions. You can discuss benefits for your client, such as how your product or service makes something stronger, lasts longer than another product, or saves the prospect money. You can explain how your product or service can make your prospect more efficient in the duties he or she must perform.

There are numerous benefits to consider and mention during the sales presentation that will help make the prospect desire what you have to offer. The obvious benefits are worthwhile to discuss because they are motivating. But there are other benefits that are more motivating than the ones we previously mentioned. These are **emotional benefits**.

Emotional benefits include things that will make the client look younger, feel more confident, have more self-esteem, and be more energetic or radiant. Always try to include these when and if they apply.

Remember, people buy based on emotion, then justify their purchase based on facts. Here's an example. A man buys a big screen television prior to the Super Bowl. He bought it because he knew he would enjoy watching the big game on a huge screen. He wanted to be the envy of his friends. But when he arrives home and is asked by his wife why he bought the television, he tells her that their old television was starting to malfunction in some way or that the TV he bought was on sale for a really good price. He bought it based on emotion, but justifies the purchase based on other facts.

If we touch our client emotionally, their decision to buy moves from their heart to their wallet. A great way to touch them emotionally is by relating a story back to the client. You can tell your prospect a story about another client who was in a similar situation, and how they overcame some obstacles and were so glad after buying your product or service. Then, tell your client that they will feel the same way the other client felt once they get the product or service.

Dr. Paul Homoly would say that prospects need to *feel* they're making the right decision. He states, "Stress words like 'you' and 'needs' often. You can say, 'What this means to you is …' Make sure you are not just selling your product or service. Emphasize that you are selling solutions, health, hope, confidence. Your potential customer is not just buying your product or service, they are buying what that product or service can do for them."

Most people giving a sales presentation will state the benefits of buying the product or service, but then leave out the risk of doing nothing. This is a crucial part that should be included in all your presentations. You see, the risk of loss is much more motivating to some than the benefit of gain.

Explain to your client how, for example, by not purchasing what you have for sale, they will be losing a lot more time by not getting a more efficient machine. Or tell them how it will cost them a lot more money by not getting your new software, which automates what they are doing every day.

In the case of my dental office, I will often explain that by not putting a crown on your tooth now, it will likely break, which will likely lead to a painful extraction. Then, to replace the missing tooth, you will have to do an implant or bridge for a price somewhere between $4,000-

$5,000. By placing a crown on the tooth *now*, we can avoid losing your tooth and save you at least $2,500. This is quite motivating for the patient!

I would often explain to clients that dental problems do not get any smaller or cheaper as time goes on. Then I would say, "What do you say we go ahead and get this done before it turns into a bigger, harder, and more expensive project for you?" Most of the time, they would agree to go ahead and get it done. Another question I liked to ask is, "How bad would you like this dental problem to get before we treat it?" The patient would then say that they don't want it to get any worse. They want it treated immediately.

By discussing the risks of doing nothing with your potential client, it creates urgency, which is vital in closing the sale. It's human nature for most of us to put off medical or dental procedures until we *need* them. If something is considered minor and we feel it is not immediate, we'll normally put it off until a later date.

It is always best to describe to your client the benefits they will get from your product or service, including the practical, health, financial, or emotional benefits. The risk of doing nothing must also be stated. If you have time constraints and you are not able to describe both the benefits and risks of doing nothing, then I would state only the risks of doing nothing. The risks have proven to be more motivating for a potential client than the benefits.

Many dentists and team members do a great job of explaining problems to their patients and how they can be handled, but they often blow it because they don't ask for the sale. The next chapter addresses your need to close the sale and get the patient to say "yes." All the work you have done with your prospect or patient up to this point is useless if you can't convert time into a sale. Practice and master this ability to "ask for the sale," and you will be astounded by how much your sales increase. Think about how many more patients you can help to feel better, chew better, look better, and be healthier if they agree to what you've proposed!

CHAPTER 7

PERSISTENCE IN ASKING FOR THE SALE

"I believe that persistent effort, supported by a character-based foundation, will enable you to get more of the things money will buy and all of the things money won't buy." – Zig Ziglar

FOR MOST PEOPLE, asking for the sale is the most uncomfortable part of the sales process. Some people will leave it out altogether. These people are getting a much lower number of prospects agreeing to buy their product or service. In this chapter, I will teach you how to ask for the sale without feeling uncomfortable. I will also convince you just how crucial it is to your sales success. By being consistent and pleasantly persistent asking for the sale, your sales conversions are sure to increase.

I want to make this abundantly clear: We should only ask for the sale once we determine that it is in the best interest of your potential client. We never attempt to close the sale with someone just to make a quick buck, even if we think we can get the sale. Professional sales training always involves the **highest in ethics and morals**. If you attempt to sell somebody something they don't want or need, you will regret it. It will come back to bite you. Plain and simple, it' wrong.

Learning how to ask for and close the sale is a very exciting part of the sale process. It's where the money is. But it is imperative to learn when to ask. Often, the prospect will drop hints that they are ready to buy. They express their interest and readiness to purchase, yet many salespeople keep giving their prepared sale talk, regardless of what their client is doing or saying, and they talk themselves back out of the sale. Don't make this mistake! It takes long enough to sell once—we don't need to have to sell twice, right?

According to Zig Ziglar, **63%** of all sales presentations end **without anyone asking** the prospect for the sale. They don't even give the potential client the chance to say "yes." The fastest way to lose business is to *not ask for it.* I believe most salespeople don't ask because they fear rejection. When we ask our patients for the sale, we are putting them on the spot. There's an awkward moment where they might say "no."

Most people tend to avoid this moment. They state their fee, and if the customer or patient doesn't jump up and say, "I'll take it, where do I pay?" they give them a copy of the estimate and tell them to call if they decide they want to buy the product or service. Unfortunately, most people are not that extroverted. They may not speak up and announce their commitment to buy. Some do, but most don't.

We must understand that just because some people don't make it clear they *want* our product, doesn't mean they *don't want* it. It all comes down to understanding what makes us comfortable enough to buy and uncomfortable enough to not buy.

Look for buying signals before you start asking your closing questions. These signals can be verbal or non-verbal. Non-verbal clues can include your prospect leaning forward or acting more attentive while you're speaking. Their eyes might widen as they hang on your every word. Nodding their head while you are speaking is another good sign. They could also smile, showing their pleasure at what they are hearing. Verbal buying signals include little sounds like "uh-huh," or "hmm," expressing their agreement or admiration.

Other verbal signs can include asking questions that someone would only ask once they have already committed to buying the product or service, such as, "How long will my warranty protect my purchase?" Your prospect might also ask you to repeat something you have explained. They may ask how soon they can expect delivery of your product. In my dental office, patients often ask if we have financing, or they want to know how long it will take to get all their work completed. These signals show interest. Once you've noticed them, you should begin the closing process of your sale.

After the fee is presented, you want to ask closing questions to get the prospect to move forward and say "yes." You always want to ask the questions in a sincere and friendly way. You can ask, "Do you want to have this done?" "How do you feel about this treatment?" or "Does this product fit your needs?" Another approach would be to ask, "Are you comfortable with that?" "How does that fit into your budget?" or "Will that work for you?"

Many salespeople like to use the "assumptive close." This is where you ask a closing question that assumes your prospect already has agreed to the purchase of your product or service. In my dental office, once I have felt the dental service was already sold, I would say, "Let's set an appointment for you to get started right away. Would this week or next week be better for you to start?" Or I would ask, "Are mornings or afternoons better for you to come in to complete the dental work we discussed today?" If they answer the question, they are sold. If they are not sold yet, they will speak up and say that they are not sure if they can do it yet. They might mention that they have to go home and "talk to their spouse," or go "think about it."

If the patient answers the closing question and says that afternoons are best for them or that next week would be good to start, then you know they are truly committed to doing the work. Next, we would have the patient pre-pay for their work and get them on the schedule to start their treatment at a convenient time for them.

My personal favorite closing question with my patients in the dental office is "What do you say we go ahead and get this done before it turns into a bigger, more expensive project for yourself?" This question asks the person for the sale while simultaneously providing urgency. It tells them what will happen if they don't get it done (risk of doing nothing).

Another good closing question is "This is the best solution I can think of, and you're going to be happy with it. I'd like to know, what do you think of it?" You can also ask, "Does this make sense to you?" or "What else are you concerned about?" If they come up with something, you answer them and calm their concerns. But if they say nothing, you can resume, "Well, good, if there is nothing else you need clarification on, are you ready to go ahead and sign up to receive the product or service?"

When you are asking for the sale, it's important to not get nervous, tense, or become more serious and less friendly or talkative. If you do, it can be a warning sign to your prospect. They may walk away without buying your product. Remember to always maintain your composure. Smile and be sincere, friendly, and helpful during your closing questions. It is very important to have self-confidence during this part of the sales process. In most cases, your prospect will buy if you believe they will.

One thing that has always helped me stay motivated to ask for the sale is keeping in mind how many wonderful ways I can improve my prospect's life with what I have to offer. If I don't ask for the sale, they can never reap the benefits of my product/service. Their lives will not be enhanced. I feel I have a moral obligation to ask for the sale so I can help them.

Think about what you would do if you were speaking to a close friend or family member about something that could truly help them. You would explain everything they need to know, how it would enhance and benefit their lives. Then you would ask if they were interested in getting it. We wouldn't hesitate with someone close to us. We would say what we are thinking, "John, this is going to help you so much, you've got to do this for yourself." We tell it how it is with our family and close friends.

When it comes to strangers or people we barely know, we feel awkward and uncomfortable asking for the sale. We don't want to be perceived as pushy, and we don't want to risk being rejected. We must always remind ourselves that we can't help them if we don't ask. Without asking, they won't say "yes" and agree to take what we are offering. Also, if they say, "no," they are **not** rejecting us personally, they are just saying "no" to the product or service … for now.

Once you ask for the sale, BE QUIET! This is crucial! He who speaks first, loses! There can often be a prolonged awkward silence after you ask a closing question. You may feel a strong urge to butt in and say something, lower the price, or start explaining why the price is justified. **Don't say a word.** If you do, it will **not** be perceived well by the prospect. Let them process and think about what you've proposed. Wait for them to respond. Most of the time, if you follow this advice, you will be happy with their response. They'll most likely commit to your service or product.

Being persistent about asking for the sale during **every** sales presentation is paramount. Granted, it is the most awkward moment, as the salesperson is putting the prospect on the spot and waiting for an answer. This is where the "fear of rejection" comes into play. Many people completely avoid this step in the sales process because of this fear. But it's something you **must** do. As Wayne Gretzky said, you miss 100% of the shots you don't take.

My coach, Howard Partridge, often said, "Nothing happens in a business until a sale is made." It is impossible to make a sale if we don't ask for it and close it. A baseball team would never win a game if every player got only to third base, never crossing home plate. Without the skill of closing the sale, your income will be greatly reduced, and your prospects won't benefit from the services and products that you are selling, which could otherwise greatly enhance or improve their lives. If you want to impact more people positively while also dramatically increasing your income, practice continually asking for the sale.

Once we master asking for the sale, we must be prepared for objections. You must be able to sort the real objections from the fake ones, and you must learn to overcome all common objections. Many amateur salespeople make the mistake of thinking that objections mean the prospect is not interested. As you will learn in the next chapter, the very opposite is true. Objections are a normal part of the sales process.

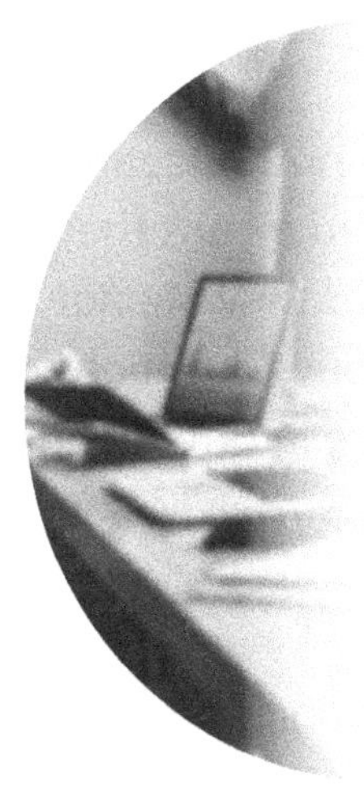

CHAPTER 8

PERSISTENCE IN OVERCOMING OBJECTIONS

"During a sales presentation, until the prospect says 'No,' assume it's a go." – Dr. Tony Matheny

WHENEVER YOU HEAR a "no" during your sales presentation, your greatest asset will be your grit and persistence. Regardless of how long you've been going to college or have worked in your field of expertise, nothing will help you overcome objections more than persistence. Overcoming is always possible, but at times it is not easy. Even the Bible has dozens of verses that inspire and encourage us to be persistent in all aspects of our life.

It is always best to try and avoid objections altogether. One way of accomplishing this is to write down all the most common objections you get to your service or product, followed by the best responses to those objections. Then, during your presentation, overcome these common objections before you can even hear them. By the end of your presentation, there will be nothing to object to. For example, if price is often an objection, you can show a testimonial letter from a previous client that states how they were concerned at first about the price, but after seeing how well the product was made and how wonderful the warranty or customer service was, they decided it was well worth it.

Most salespeople feel that objections are bad signs—that their potential client is not interested. Usually, it's the **exact opposite**.

It can show buying *intention*. If your prospect is not objecting to anything during your sales presentation, it often means they are not qualified to buy your product or service or they are not paying attention. Either way, they are not going to buy. Objections can be a sign of interest. The prospect needs more information, more time to figure it out, or more time to talk themselves into the purchase.

People are afraid of making a bad buying decision, getting scammed, or being taken advantage of. Objections allow them to delay or slow down the buying process without feeling as pressured. As Tom Hopkins says in his book, *How to Master the Art of Selling*, "Objections are the rungs of the ladder to sales success."

Great salespeople realize that the sales process doesn't start until they get their first objection or hear their first "no." A small percentage of people will immediately come in ready to buy whatever you have available. And there will be people who, after hearing your presentation for the first time, will take it right away, no questions asked. I hope you realize, from what we previously discussed, that these people are in the minority, not the majority.

With these people, sales skills aren't necessary, and you don't have to be persistent. If you stick only with these people, you will make some sales, but you will not come close to your full potential. That's why dentists only have a 25-30% acceptance rate with patients—because we were never taught sales training in dental school, and we never want to be perceived as pushy. Instead, we walk away at the first objection or the first time we hear "no."

If we want to help the other 70-75% of patients who walk out of our office, not getting the treatment they want and need, we must be persistent and apply the strategies discussed in this chapter. When we hear that first "no," we need to use our skills to work around it to get a "yes" instead. We need to realize and understand that sales of all shapes and sizes involve rejection, opposition, and difficulty.

Most people new to sales hate the thought of getting an objection. They feel it means their prospect is not interested, doesn't like them or the product, or can't afford it. But seasoned salespeople know this couldn't be further from the truth—that the opposite is actually true! Objections are often a sign of interest. If someone is not objecting to anything, they likely are not engaged. You'll learn as I did to love objections. They announce your prospect's buying intention.

Objections are the feedback we need before closing our potential client. With objections, we are given a chance to hear what is holding a prospect back from buying our product or service. We know now that we must address and overcome their concerns to get them closer to buying. I view their pushback as an incredible opportunity, which is why I don't mind objections.

When I hear an objection, I know the prospect is following along, fully engaged in our conversation and listening to everything. When they object, it often means they need more information or clarification about what we proposed. They just need more information to talk themselves into the purchase.

The reason so many people hate hearing objections is because they take them personally. They feel that the prospect is rejecting them, and they feel as though they have failed, which is simply **not true**. As I stated earlier, you need to realize that if your buyer says "no," they are not rejecting you—they are just rejecting the sale **at that specific time**. And when they say "no," it usually is not "no" forever. Remember, an objection is not *your* failure. It is *their* loss.

I like to think of objections as stones jutting out of the water in a stream, spread out two feet apart. These are the necessary steps we must take to get where we are going. People naturally have a lot of resistance when it comes to buying. In fact, Zig Ziglar says, "At least 74% of buyers will voice at least three objections before they buy." Buyers are very often afraid of making a bad buying decision. They need time and information to talk themselves into the purchase. It takes time to build in them that warm and fuzzy feeling one gets while buying. Every objection you overcome gets you one step closer to "yes." It is helpful to think of a "no" as a challenge, **not** a rejection. Just keep going. Pleasant persistence is key, so **do not give up too early**!

Before we go further into detail about handling objections with persistence, there is one crucial fact we must realize: not all objections are truthful or real. For example, a prospect might tell us that they have no money to buy our product or service, yet they have a Rolex on their wrist, we saw the fancy car they drove up in, or they just got done telling us about the long vacation they recently returned from. We obviously know it's not the money.

Knowing that this objection is not valid, what do most salespeople do? They begin discussing financing options to make the purchase easier to afford. But in this situation, the salesperson is not addressing the real concern. If we know that the objection is unlikely to be real, we are better off not trying to solve it.

It can be hard at times distinguishing a valid objection from an invalid one. How can you tell if something is true and should be handled or untrue and dealt with another way? When you ask for the sale and the prospect answers quickly, without taking any time to think about it, they are likely experiencing a knee-jerk reaction. It usually is not valid.

For example, if I tell a patient that they need three crowns done on their teeth and the investment is $3,000, then the patient immediately says, "I can't afford that," it is often not true. But why would they say it if it wasn't true? For several reasons. One is that they were caught off guard, surprised by the fee and were expecting the cost to be lower than it is. When someone feels overwhelmed, they often can't think straight. They blurt out statements like this to get away from the situation.

Another reason might be that the patient is not sold yet on the fact they need the service. They may need more information about the benefits of doing the crowns or the risks of not doing them to talk themselves into the procedure.

The best way to respond to someone who gives you a very quick response or objection is to not try and solve their objection (because you know it's likely not valid). What you should do is acknowledge the objection to let them know that you heard them, then mention another benefit of doing the procedure or the risk of doing nothing. Next, ask for the sale again and see what they say. They will give one of three responses. They will either give the same objection again, give another objection you haven't heard yet, or agree to take the service you are recommending.

In my crown example above, if I mention the fee is $3,000 and the patient says, "I can't afford that!" I'd respond by saying, "I hear you" or "I realize it's a big investment, but let me share this with you." Then I'd explain a benefit of doing the work or risk of not doing it. Next, I would ask for the sale again, saying something like, "Doesn't it make sense to get it done now before it gets worse or more expensive?" The patient would come back with one of the three responses in the paragraph above. If they give the same objection, I will treat the objection of not having enough money as valid and would talk about financing options. If they object in a different manner, I'd repeat the process by acknowledging the objection, stating another benefit or risk, and asking for the sale again. This process repeats until they say "yes" or "no."

On the other hand, you may encounter a patient who is sincerely trying to figure out a way to afford the crowns and work the treatment into their budget. But, after a few moments, they express how they simple can't afford it. In this case, I would discuss financing options immediately, because their objection seems credible.

Most salespeople never get down to the real objection because they have not had proper sales training. They assume that if they get an objection, it is always true and valid, and they attempt to overcome the objection the only way they know how. Luckily, we know the difference between real and fake objections.

A common objection—and one of the hardest to overcome—is "I have to think it over." Other versions of this can be, "Let me sleep on it," or "Give me the information or estimate and I will get back to when I've made a decision." Most salespeople simply stop their sales presentation when they hear one of these responses. They feel they will be perceived as too pushy or aggressive if they continue, so they move on. If you do this, the prospect will rarely ever "think it over" and get back to you. In most circumstances, this objection is simply a stall, not the true objection. They will likely avoid the sale.

So, in this situation, you must immediately follow the advice from earlier in this chapter. You must discern whether the objection is valid or not. Following this advice, we simply say, "I understand you wanting to think it over, but let me share this with you." Then you give them another benefit of taking the service or product, or another risk of doing nothing. Next, you ask them a closing question to get the commitment and sale from the prospect. Often, they will go ahead and say, "yes." And then you are done!

They may also give you a different objection. If they do, repeat the above process until they either commit or say "no." They might even say, "I never make commitments like this on the spot, I am someone who has to weigh all the options, then decide." At this point, I would inquire more about what is it they have to think about. Are they not sure about your company, or concerned with making the procedure fit it into their schedule? Often, it is the price—but no one wants to admit that. If you find out it is price, you can discuss financing options.

When objections from a client are piling up, I'll often ask, "So I know what to put in the chart, what is it exactly you want to think about? Are you not sure if you want me to do the work on you?" Following that, they always say, "No, I'd feel comfortable having you be my dentist." I follow up with, "Are you not sure that you really want or need the procedure?" They'll say, "No, I am sure I need it." After two or three of these questions (where the answer is always "no"), they often speak up and say, "It's the cost."

Now I know the true objection. Next, tell them, "To clarify, this treatment is something you would go forward with if we can work it into your budget on a monthly basis?" Upon hearing "yes," you can start discussing financing options. Don't ask if money is the true issue. Most of the time, they'll simply deny it, and a bigger issue will have been created.

Another common objection is "the price is too high" or "I can't afford it." Just like with the previous objection, you want to make sure this objection is true and valid. Acknowledge that you heard what they are saying by stating, "I understand it is a significant investment, but let me share this with you." Then, state another benefit of buying the service or product, or a risk of not buying it. (Don't forget how powerful the emotional benefits can be.)

Next, ask for the sale again and attempt to close. Often, they will go ahead and take what you are offering. If they object further, repeat the process. If they repeat the objection of the price being too high or say they can't afford it, share some of the statements listed below.

First, try asking "Just to clarify, would you definitely buy it if the price was lower?" This may bring out another objection you need to address. You can ask if this is the type of service or product they would get if they could work it into their budget in monthly installments. If they say "yes," you can discuss various finance options. Another thing I'll often ask is, "What makes you feel it is too expensive?" They might be comparing a different, similar product to yours. Once you know that, you may be able to distinguish how much better your product/service is when it comes to quality, service, warranty, longevity, etc.

In my dental office, I would say, "Yes, we do cost more than some other dental offices. Thank goodness for that! Our costs help us provide you with the highest quality restorations by using the best materials and dental laboratories, as well as top customer service. We believe in excellence. You get what you pay for!" I'll also state, "We cannot be the best and the cheapest." People often complain about the money, even though they could easily afford it. They might not be sold yet, but in most cases, they just likely think the product should be cheaper because of what they've heard in the past or from someone else.

In this case, explain to your clients that you had a choice when you started your company. You could have used the cheapest material, spent less time making the product, and not stood behind what you believed in. Instead, you chose to not cut corners, charged a little more than average, used the best materials, took the time to do it right, and stood behind what you believed in. You can tell your client, "I'm glad I chose the second option, aren't you?" Tell your prospect that "nothing good is cheap and nothing cheap is good."

When a patient would respond, "Wow, that's a lot," or "You guys are expensive," I would explain that we are not the *most* or *least* expensive office in town. I would explain that the investment reflects the above-average care we offer. I would also state, "Every dentist knows what his/her dentistry is worth. Our goal is to provide the absolute highest quality dentistry possible, at a fee that is average or slightly above."

If you really want to get your client thinking, tell them, "The investment you pay now for our product or service will be less than what you will pay later if you don't go forward now." Half of the time, you will not be able to overcome the "price is too high" objection. But that still leaves 50% of people who will go forward and say "yes" after initially complaining about the price being too high.

Even though there are several objections a potential client can give, we will cover one more. We hear this objection often: "I have to talk to my spouse." Just like we did with the previous objections, make sure it is a valid objection. I would tell my clients, "I understand you want to talk to your spouse, but let me share this with you." Then I'd provide another benefit of getting the service/product or mention another risk of doing nothing. But most importantly, you must not forget to ask for the sale again. Many times, they will go ahead and commit to taking what you are offering. If they bring this objection up a second time, offer them some validity and start to ask more questions.

Before I go into what I'd say in response to this objection, keep in mind that the best strategy is to avoid this objection in the first place by trying to have the spouse in the room during the sales presentation. When you make an appointment with the prospect, ask, "Is there anyone else that you usually confer with in making decisions like this?" It is crucial to have all the decision-makers in the room. It is always best for both spouses to hear all the information firsthand. This way, you can answer their questions together, overcome any objections, and hopefully reach an agreement on the spot to move forward with your product/service.

Getting the spouse in the room is often not possible due to work-related reasons. If this is the case, I will ask if their spouse is available by phone for me to speak with for a few minutes. Then I'll give the spouse a brief summary of what their wife/husband needs and why, go over the benefits of doing the service and the risks of doing nothing, state the price, handle any objections, and ask for the sale. Most of the time, they will say to put their spouse on the phone to tell them it is okay to pay and make an appointment.

If the spouse is not available by phone at that time, I will ask permission to call later that night (when they are finished work). If I am not able to talk to them at all that day, I'll try to schedule another time to speak with the spouse. And if that is still not feasible, make sure the person in front of you is very clear on why they need your service or product. List all the benefits, and make sure they are sold on it before they go home to talk to their spouse. Usually, the sale will be completed if the prospect properly understands why they need your service, as they will then communicate that information to their spouse.

For those times when it is not possible for the spouse to come in, you can say, "If you were the only one making the decision here, would you go ahead and get it?" If they say anything but "yes," ask more questions and overcome their objections until they are in full agreement.

Once they agree and express their happiness and willingness to go forward, and if it was just them deciding, you can ask, "Does this mean you'll be recommending this product or service to your spouse?" It's good to have one spouse give their approval or express how much they need or want your product or service—but **don't have them give the sales presentation for you!** This rarely goes well. You are way better off arranging a time to meet with the spouse who couldn't be there originally. At least get them on the phone to talk yourself.

In some cases, someone will say they have to speak with their spouse because there is a price objection (though they likely won't admit this). You can say, "From my experience, when someone says they want to talk to their spouse, they are often concerned with the price. Is this the case with you?" If they acknowledge there is a price objection, financing options can be discussed.

One final tip for overcoming objections: use stories. Share with your prospect a story about another customer who felt the same way they felt. Then tell them how this client had faith and went forward with the purchase, and how it improved their life dramatically. People love stories—they relate to them. They will remember them much more than facts you share. According to Dan and Chip Heath, bestselling authors of *Made to Stick*, after a presentation, 63% of attendees remember stories. Only 5% remember statistics. When your prospect can see how others have overcome similar obstacles, they'll be more prone to purchase what you're selling.

No matter how good you are at presenting your product or service, there will always be people you will not be able to get to commit.

But don't fear! They might not say "yes" at the time, but that doesn't mean you can't ultimately get the sale at a future meeting or another time down the road. It is all dependent on your "follow-up." Don't underestimate the power and success of a persistent follow-up. We will go over this in detail in the next chapter.

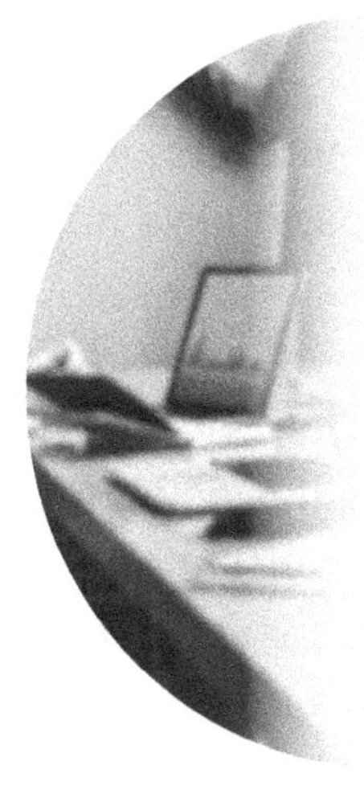

CHAPTER 9

PERSISTENCE IN YOUR FOLLOW-UP

"80% of sales require five follow-up calls after the meeting. 44% of sales reps give up after one follow-up." – The Brevet Group

YOU'VE LIKELY HEARD the expression in real estate that the three most important things are location, location, location. In sales, those three things are follow-up, follow-up, follow-up. Follow-up is just another way of saying persistence. The better your follow-up, the better your sales success will be. It is the absolute secret to success. This stage of the selling process is often skipped by people in sales. Worse, many salespeople outright fear it.

At the core of their fear is the idea they're going to annoy their prospect, become too aggressive, or be seen as a spammer. Some don't want to be perceived as following up too much. Or they fear rejection so much, they avoid the possibility of hearing a definitive "no." Personally, I don't mind hearing a "no!" At least a "no" shows where they stand. I can move on to someone else who may be more interested in what I have to offer. Also, the person who gave you the "no" is probably closer than ever before to buying. If you stick in there a little while longer, they might say "yes" instead.

If you are truly sincere, genuine, and helpful with your follow up, your potential client will not get the feeling you are harassing or hounding them. It is all about being "pleasantly persistent." It is imperative to your sales success to be very diligent and persevere through your follow-up method. Don't quit. It will pay off in a big way.

48% of people **never** follow up with their prospect. If you don't include the follow-up as part of your sales process, it is going to be difficult for you to succeed in sales. When you get rejected, just look at it as if you just got one out of the five rejections you need to get the client to say "yes." Failing to follow up is a sure way of losing up to **80%** of your potential sales, according to Ian Loew's article, *The Art of the Sales Follow-Up: 7 Ways to Keep the Conversation Going*. That can result in a significant loss of revenue for you. Don't feel as if you are annoying or pressuring your prospect by following up with them. Instead, you are being persistent because what you offer can help your prospect fulfill a need or solve their problem.

When your prospect is ready to buy, you need to be there for them. Position yourself as the best option. You do this through consistent follow-ups. There is **no other way**. Your buyer will trust you the **more** they see you, hear you, or have any other form of contact with you.

As we have seen, not many people will buy on their first, second, or even third exposure to your product or service. Knowing that, it really shouldn't be our goal on first attempt with a new client to make the sale. Your plan should be to build a relationship and develop trust. Build dialogue and get to know each other more. A great example of this is dating. You wouldn't ask someone to marry you on the first date. You want to get your date to like you and go on a second date with you, then a third date. Eventually, a proposal might come.

Since only 2% of sales will close on the first meeting, you must continue reaching out to your prospect. Making one or two sales calls will usually NOT get you the sale. You must keep following up with the prospect until they are open to buying. It is crucial that you be persistent, not in an annoying or stalking way, but with drive and motivation.

Most potential buyers will not be ready to commit to making a purchase when they are first approached by a salesperson. There are several reasons why this is the case: the prospect may not have the time to talk, they may not have the resources to make a decision, or they may have to do some research first. They also may not have the authority to make a decision. Perhaps they need permission from someone first.

Instead of trying to make a sale on the first call, it could work well to try to implement a follow-up strategy. This allows you to engage in an ongoing dialogue with your customer, creating trust and building a relationship.

When you think about it, it makes sense most sales don't occur the first meeting. You have **not** built any trust or any type of relationship. You haven't had enough time with your prospect yet to find out what their needs are and how your product or service can help meet those needs. During your first meeting, the prospect could have been having a bad day, been distracted, had some recent financial difficulties, or may have been late for another engagement. Who knows? All we know for certain is that they were not able to commit to saying "yes" at that time.

By building this relationship, you'll understand the needs and wants of your client. You'll get to know the real objections they have with a product or service, not the initial reasons they gave when they first met you. As soon as the client feels that you truly understand them and hear them, you will have a customer for life. They will doubt that anyone else will be committed to investing the time and energy that you did.

If you are satisfied with just one follow-up and you continue to rely on the prospect to return your follow-up, you are missing revenue opportunities. Usually, decisions are **not** made quickly. That's why you must continue managing the sales process. It takes some effort and time to build the needed relationship. To compete in your market, your presence and professional persistence will make all the difference.

The very first step towards being professionally persistent—without being an annoyance—is to make any communications you have with your prospect highly relevant to them. It is better to get in touch with them less while relaying *high-quality messages*, rather than contact them frequently with spammy, unimportant messages.

Again, it is crucial to be pleasantly persistent. You must set up a specific date to follow up with the prospect. By setting a deadline, it tends to minimize any indecision or ambiguity, which allows the salesperson to control the timetable. Being persistent can lead to referrals, repeat business, and a request for other products and/or services.

Potential clients will often reward your persistence with a sale. If not, they will remember how persistent you were and—in the future and when/if their situation changes—it will be *you* they come back to for the sale. According to the National Sales Executive Association, **48% of salespeople never follow up** with their prospects. I would not recommend giving up on a prospect until I was rejected at **least four times**.

Even then, I would probably keep their contact information. After a break of three-six months, I would reach out again. Not to ask for the sale, but to check in and see how they were doing. I don't want them to forget my name and what I do. Once you have identified your prospect, be very persistent and diligent in following up and pursuing them through various channels. I would follow up through email, telephone, social media, forums/events, private messaging, or in person. When you do reach out, consider notifying them of a special offer or a limited-time discount. This can really help you reengage with a prospect you haven't spoken to recently.

Make sure you provide value with each follow-up. Your prospects know you are selling them something, but they don't want to feel as if they are being subjected to an aggressive sales pitch. This type of hard selling simply does not work anymore. You will get better results if you can make sure you are providing great value and your prospect is engaged. Just make sure your conversation is all about **them**, not about you or your product. Keeping notes from first contact with your prospect can be very helpful during these follow-ups. And remember, you are not selling a product or service, you are **selling a solution** to a problem.

When following up with your prospect, you must define what the next step in the process is. This is one of the biggest mistakes salespeople make. Don't ever rely on your prospect to call you back after they "check with their spouse" or "have to think about it." Make a specific time and date for when you will follow up with them. Say, "I will call you back Tuesday night at 7:30."

The type of system or template you come up with to help organize how and when you will follow up could be the difference between you making or not making a sale. If you don't have or refuse to make a follow-up system, be okay with the fact that you will have a lot less sales. A great follow-up system is crucial. Custom design a system that you are comfortable with, applies to your business, and which you will be consistent following after every sale.

Email is one method to follow-up with your potential client. An advantage of this method is that your customer has written copy of their estimate, along with everything you are recommending in front of them to print out to review and show their spouse. The disadvantage of this method is that your customer may not even see it due to the enormous amount of junk mail they get every day. They may also delete it after reading the subject line, thinking it is nothing that interests or applies to them.

When you send an email, try to always include these three points: First, tell your client why you are contacting them, which focuses on him or her; second, tell them why you are reaching out at the *specific* time you've contacted them; and third, ask for a short action you want them to take, a call to action, such as agreeing to a follow-up call or to meet for a free consultation.

With email follow-ups, the subject line is critical. Don't make the error in writing a generic subject line like, "Just following up," or "Checking in with you." People get so many junk emails today, and subject lines that lack passion can easily be deleted. You only have a few seconds to grab their attention and make them want to open your email. According to research compiled by Pinpoint Marketing, you can increase the open rate of your emails by about **30%** by including the name of your prospect in the subject line. And over **60%** of people say they open their email based on how relevant the subject line title is.

Here are some ideas for creating great subject line emails:

- Create a sense of urgency. State a specific time the follow-up must occur by, or mention a limited-time offer.
- Demonstrate value in the subject by saying something like "I recently read this article and I thought it would be helpful for you."

- Ask a direct question to arouse curiosity, such as: "Wait until you read this," "What do you think about _____?" or "Can you help me out with ____ please?"

Another great idea is to include a link to a video, blog post, or relevant article that strongly relates to the problems your prospect is having. When you provide them with this useful content, you show how much you care. You show how interested you are in a mutually beneficial relationship. Try to keep your email brief—around six lines or less is a good guideline.

Making a phone call can be more personal and establish you as a human instead of a spam-bot. Try to keep this call brief. If you are comfortable being on the phone, you can make a connection quicker than you would through email. The downside of making a call is that it is hard to reach people nowadays. Most of the time, you will get the person's voicemail. And if you leave a voicemail, you can't assume that it will be heard or that you'll receive a response.

The best solution to getting in touch with your clients or potential clients is to phone them and email them. Alternate between the two until you reach them. Then you can review what you discussed, provide any new information, mention benefits of your product or service, risks of not going forward, and maybe even ask them for that all-important sale!

If you don't get a response after emailing and phoning, wait 48 hours and then try reaching out again. Tell them that you have been trying to reach them. Try another approach this time.

After three attempts to reach them without any response, I would send one more email and/or call one more time. Tell them once again that you have been trying to reach them but haven't had any success. Explain how you don't want to bother them if there's no fit between them and your company. Tell them you will not be contacting them in the future, but you are always there to help them when they are ready. Funnily enough, most salespeople will tell you that this "break-up" email is the one that gets the most responses. People don't want to be taken out of your system. They will often reach out, saying they just need a little more time.

Don't forget about social media. By interacting with your clients on social media, you can sway them toward speaking with you. Find creative ways to contact your client. Since we know it takes, on average, five contacts to get the sale, we can reach that magic number in various ways. You might arrange a visit, send an email, make a phone call, leave a note, text them, or engage on social media.

You can also send them a letter. By combining ways to contact the client, you can reach five contacts without appearing like a stalker. You can see **double** the success rate when you use **two** communication methods. When you add a third method, you can see an increase of an **extra 3-5%**. Multiple touch points repeated two or three times can really benefit the relationship between you and your client, potentially leading to a sale. (This statistic comes directly from my dental office, where we saw the success of multiple contact methods.)

During the follow-up with your client over the phone, try not to rush through the call. For every additional minute you are on the phone, you multiply your odds of success with the client by **SIX**. How? Because you have time to explain the products or services your company has to offer. You have a chance to find out more of what the client wants or needs. You should take this time to really listen to the client. The client can also explain what their concerns or limitations are before buying what you are offering. Spending extra time with the client makes Ithem feel like you really understand them. And once that happens, you have forged a bond with them.

If you get to voicemail when you do a follow-up call, it is okay to leave a message. Especially if your prospect has shown interest when you first got together, you have some new, valuable information that could benefit them, or you got a lot of positive feedback from them when you spoke previously. I do not suggest leaving a message on voicemail if you haven't talked to the prospect before and have no relationship with them.

Don't forget about an old school method: sending a handwritten letter. It goes a long way with people. Taking the time to handwrite a note and mail it leaves a lasting impression. It's one of the sincerest forms of following up, and you can give them more information or thank them for taking the time to meet or speak with you.

Years ago, when I first moved to Florida, I became certified in scuba diving. One day, I went into a local dive shop and purchased all the dive equipment I needed. The owner was not in the store when I bought the equipment. A couple days later, I received a handwritten note from the owner thanking me for my business. He told me to contact him personally if I needed anything else. I was so impressed. He'd taken time out of his busy schedule to thank me for my business. He already had my money—he didn't have to thank me. That was over 20 years ago, and here I am still talking about it. Talk about a lasting impression, huh? Do you think I would go back there if I needed more dive equipment? You bet!

There are some rules to follow that can improve the process of any follow-up. These rules will ultimately increase the odds of securing a sale. One thing you can do is provide them with more content. When you express to the client that you discovered new information that may help them, they will be more receptive to what you have to say.

Here's another rule. When you talk to the client, be sure to work into the conversation the key points most relevant to them—those that he/she has expressed previously during your question-asking period. Another rule is to be very friendly. Don't be afraid to inject some humor. Making them laugh helps build rapport. Sell benefits more than features, especially emotional benefits. And always attempt to close the sale by asking for it.

In my dental office, when I would call a patient to follow up on a treatment plan we previously discussed, I would often say things like, "I was thinking about you today and wanted to share something with you that I forgot to tell you last time," or "I realized today that I forgot to mention a couple things when we last talked. This information might help with your decision."

After saying one of these lines, I mention another benefit of doing the treatment or another risk of doing nothing. Sometimes, I tell them, "I know we went over a lot of information during your last visit. I wanted to see if I could answer any new questions you or your spouse might have?"

When I ask if they have any questions, sometimes they tell me, "No, we can go ahead and make an appointment to get the work done." I am always surprised by this. They didn't agree to do the work when they were in my office last time, so I didn't expect them to agree now to do it. If they changed their mind and decided to do it, why hadn't they picked up the phone and called me to schedule the work? Some people are willing to but just haven't taken the time or initiative to call yet. It's always amazing to me how that works.

In the past, I've sent a letter to a patient who hadn't been in my office for eight years. She ended up calling and made an appointment to come in to get some much-needed dental work done. She said even though she hadn't been into the office in a long time, she never forgot about us. When she got our letter, it was the perfect time for her to come in.

Another patient called to tell us that she had to go to another dentist in town because her insurance changed, and she could no longer use her dental insurance in our office. She went on to say that she received a birthday card from our office and that our card was the only one she received on her birthday. It touched her so much, she made an appointment to come in, even though she had to pay out of pocket. That's the power of the follow-up! **Never give up!**

In his book *The Sales Bible*, Jeffrey H. Gitomer says, "If there were a formula for following up, it would be ... new information + creative + sincere + direct + friendly + humor = SALE ... but there isn't an exact formula."

When you follow up with your prospect, you are indeed being **persistent**. You are not giving up on the sale. Potential clients need time to talk themselves into the sale and work out any resistance they're fighting in their head. They want to be convinced and feel as sure as they can that they are not making a bad decision. Spend the time to follow up, and it will truly yield great results.

CHAPTER 10

SUMMARY/CLOSING COMMENTS

"I believe that persistent effort, supported by a character-based foundation, will enable you to get more of the things money will buy and all of the things money won't buy." – Zig Ziglar

SELLING IN A pleasantly persistent manner can greatly increase your sales success, helping lead to the Three R's: repeat business, referrals, and requests for additional products or services.

Determination and resolve will win you more sales. If your goal is long-term success, you must be persistent. Keep your name at the front of your client's mind.

Consistency leads to familiarity, familiarity leads to trust, and trust leads to action. Action turns your prospects into clients. Remember, persistence is all about not giving up even when it feels like the best choice. Don't get down or discouraged if it takes more time than you thought to close a deal. In the end, it will be worth it!

When it comes to sales, your persistence and grit in the face of hearing "no" is your greatest asset. A resilient mindset will get you through your sales journey. It doesn't matter how many degrees you have, how many years you have been working in the field, or how much money you have. It all comes down to "who is willing to persist."

Many people fail to persist, and they even look down upon those who do. This is often due to the confusion between sales *persistence* and sales *pressure*. With sales persistence, you empathize, adjust, and move forward with a new message or solution. You create more value or come up with a new approach. In contrast, sales pressure communicates the same thing over and over with disregard to the prospect's worries, concerns, or fears.

There are four main reasons why it is crucial for you to be persistent with selling. The first reason is that people simply may want or need more to commit and buy what you're offering. People are skeptical and afraid to make a bad buying decision. If they're initially resistant, give them more value. Remember, the value must exceed the price in **their** mind. If you give them a big enough reason, they will commit and go forward with the sale.

Second, some people just need to hear your proposal a different way. What is motivating and makes one person feel comfortable to buy can be completely different than what makes another prospect comfortable. You need to keep reframing and repositioning your message until it resonates enough with your potential client or customer. You'll make the sale once you deliver the right message the right way. Doing so takes persistence.

Third, some people don't commit initially because they don't know how to work through all the steps necessary to go forward with what you are proposing. It's overwhelming to them. Remember, if they get overwhelmed or confused, they often walk away. But if we lay things out for them step by step, holding their hand along the way, they'll feel secure enough to go forward with the sale. This takes persistence. You must get your prospect to understand the process, and they must understand that you will be there with them to assist and guide them.

Finally, we need to be persistent because some people just need more time to figure it all out. These types need to convince themselves that it is a good idea and good value, that the benefits are worth it, and that the risk of loss is great if they don't go forward with the sale. The amount of time it takes for your prospect to know you, like you, and trust you enough to go forward can be anywhere from a couple days to a few years. Everyone is different, and everyone's situation is unique and constantly evolving.

A "no" today doesn't mean a "no" tomorrow, next week, month, or year. In my dental office, there have been times when I've told a patient they need cleaning work done twice a year every year, but they don't agree to the treatment. I'm always shocked by this. However, by being persistent and continuing to stress the importance of these cleanings, they finally agree, schedule, and pay for the treatment. You never know why or what changed with them, and you don't care. You're just glad they are going to get healthier. Remember, asking a prospect again at a different time might bring a totally different response.

After acquiring a new client, many salespeople forget to ask for referrals. Renowned author Dale Carnegie once stated that **91%** of people said they would be willing to give a referral, but **only 11% actually ask for them**. The best time to ask for a referral is right after your client gives you, your team, or your product or service a compliment. In my dental office, if a patient said, "I love my new smile," I would say, "Thanks so much! Do you have a friend or family member who could benefit from the dental work we do here?"

I also ask for referrals after I've trained a dentist and their team on how to sell more dentistry. I'll say, "Do you know of any other dentists who would like to collect more while reducing stress and the number of patients they have to see each day?" I'll try to get one or two names and numbers, then ask them to tell the people they are referring to you that you'll be calling (or ask for a personal introduction). Remember, it's a numbers game. The more referrals you ask for, the more you will receive. It costs nothing, and these people already come to you with some level of rapport and trust due to the person who referred them. The odds of getting these referrals to purchase your products or services are much higher than with strangers. Be persistent asking for referrals. You'll be happy you did—the numbers will speak for themselves.

I loved this quote from my mentor, Zig Ziglar, "One difference between those who make it and those who don't—regardless of their field of endeavor—is not the 'talent' difference. Those who go over the top have a dream and the dream has them. They make the commitment and pursue that dream with dogged patience and persistence. Commitment produces consistent, enthusiastic effort that inevitably produces greater and greater rewards."

All we have to do is look to children to see how important persistence is to the sales process. We've all seen a little kid (perhaps even our own children) in the grocery store wanting a piece of candy, the parent saying "no," and the kid dropping to the ground, kicking and screaming, throwing a temper tantrum. You don't see the child giving up after their first "no" do you? After saying, "Please, please, please, Mom, I'll be good all day, I need the candy, Mom, please!" Mom usually gives in and buys their child the candy. We perfected the art of persistence as children. But somehow, we forgot or lost these skills when we became adults who own businesses.

In this book, we covered several of the most crucial elements you'll want to practice, and eventually master, to increase your sales success. These included being persistent with your mindset first, followed by persistence in prospecting, preparation, questioning, giving benefits and risks, asking for the sale, overcoming objections, and the follow-up. I just want to stress again that you can't learn them once and think you've mastered them for life. You must practice and review them constantly. It's too easy to revert to old habits. Practice regularly, and I believe you'll agree—as I did—that this will be the greatest skill you have ever learned!

Being persistent is the most important trait to perfect during sales presentations. It won't always be easy. Don't be like most people and give up way too early, right when your prospect is finally ready to buy. You should be there to take their order! It usually takes between five and seven "nos" to get the sale. The only way you can get through all these "nos" to reach a "yes" is by being persistent. If you continually adjust your approach, empathize with your prospect, and create new approaches and better messages, you will achieve success beyond your dreams. Any seasoned or professional salesperson will answer, when asked about the key to their sales success, that **persistence** was key. Hopefully, you see now just how crucial it is to **always be pleasantly persistent**!

HOW TO LEARN MORE FROM DR. MATHENY

ALTHOUGH THIS BOOK taught many tips and strategies to help you achieve better sales numbers, there is a lot of information that didn't fit zin. Especially for dentists, there are crucial concepts to learn and master for great sales success. These include:

*How to match the prospect's emotional state, be authentic, and have them follow your lead.

*The key things you must have in place to have the highest odds of success.

*How to provide social proof so your prospect trusts what you are telling them.

*How to overcome all the objections we hear, including "need to think about it," "talk to spouse," "no money," "too old," "no time," "scared," "price too high," and "only want to do what insurance covers."

*Principles of great sales (case) presentations and traits of a good presenter.

*How to lose and gain rapport with your prospect.

*How patient education can hurt case acceptance.

*Words not to use with your patients.

*How to properly perform a clinical exam and discuss the problems and options with the patient.

*How to give the cost of the dental treatment in a way that doesn't shock or overwhelm the patient, but instead allows them to feel relieved and figure out a way of getting it done.

*How to prevent "buyer's remorse" and have your patients not call for a refund because they changed their mind.

*How to sell high-end dentures despite there being more inexpensive denture clinics in town.

*How to sell cosmetic dentistry that nobody *needs* to be healthy, but which they may still want.

*How to be profitable with PPOs.

*How to sell more costly porcelain inlay and onlay restorations as opposed to composite.

*Tons of examples applying these strategies to the dental office, plus so much more!

As you can see, there is tons more to learn. The more you can add to your sales skillset, the better your results will be. Think of yourself as a contractor with a tool belt. Every skill you master is another tool in your sales tool belt! You can use these skills if and when the circumstance presents itself. The more tools you add, the more your business will succeed and grow.

A great no-cost option to learn more about increasing your case acceptance through ethical selling—an option that will teach you to not be aggressive, pushy, or high pressure—is to sign up for one of Dr. Matheny's FREE Challenges. Go to his website, **www.drtonymatheny.com**, to learn more, or check one of his social media pages listed below.

Dr. Matheny has developed other programs that will help you achieve sales mastery, obtain the best results, and achieve your goals. The ultimate learning experience is coaching from Dr. Matheny himself. This is done in his **Case Acceptance Mastery Coaching Program**. It is a 12-week program that includes lifetime access to the entire program on video, plus an hour-long call every week to teach that week's material and have a Q&A session. It is a Do-It-With-You approach. This program makes it easy for you to learn the material you need to succeed, and it holds you accountable and helps to ensure your success! At the end of the 12 weeks the program repeats from the beginning. This means you can hear the material multiple times, helping with retention and magnifying results.

To discuss if you would be a good fit for this program, email Dr. Matheny at the email below. We can set up a time to talk about your needs. During this call, you'll see how you can learn to dramatically increase your case acceptance and collect more, while also decreasing your stress and the volume of people you must see each day.

If the coaching program is not a possibility for you, the online video course—called **Doctor Sales Academy**—can be purchased separately. This program covers all aspects of sales training and is specifically tailored to the dental office with tons of real-life examples. This option is good for people who possess the discipline to watch the videos on their own and practice the strategies and techniques they've learned independently. It is a Do-It-Yourself type of approach. To learn more about this option, go to www.drtonymatheny.com

and, under Courses, click Doctor Sales Academy. You can email Dr. Matheny with any questions at **info@drtonymatheny.com**, or you can visit his website.

Many have asked how to get the patient to pay in advance after they've said "yes." To address these requests, Dr. Matheny developed his **Show Me the Money Masterclass**. This course includes 10 videos that cover several aspects of collecting the money upfront, including what to say to get the patient to pre-pay, handling objections to prepaying, dealing with insurance and pre-authorizations, preventing buyer's remorse, and much more. You can check this out at www.drtonymatheny.com under the Courses tab as well. Or you can email him.

Dr. Matheny is also available to speak at your dental society meeting or convention at the local, state, and national levels. He can give presentations ranging from 30 minutes to two full days. Your attendees can learn why sales training is the most beneficial skill to improve their dental offices, how to tell if objections are real or false, how to overcome all the objections we face as dentists, how to close the sale to get the commitment from the patient, how to present the fees in a way that doesn't shock or overwhelm the patient, and how to follow up.

Dr. R. Anthony Matheny

Website: www.drtonymatheny.com
Email: info@drtonymatheny.com
Toll-free number: (844) 366-4004

Facebook: **https://www.facebook.com/drtonymatheny**

Facebook Page for Doctor Sales Academy:
https://www.facebook.com/Doctor-Sales-Academy-107934854260074

Instagram: https://www.instagram.com/dr.tonymatheny/

LinkedIn: https://www.linkedin.com/in/drmatheny/

www.ingramcontent.com/pod-product-compliance
Lightning Source LLC
Chambersburg PA
CBHW060622200326
41521CB00007B/862